OPEN
EDUCATION
A Beginning

OPEN EDUCATION

A Beginning

ANNE BREMER|JOHN BREMER

HOLT, RINEHART AND WINSTON
New York Chicago San Francisco

Library of Congress Catalog Card Number: 76-190278

ISBN: 0-03-086117-9 (Paper)

ISBN: 0-03-091921-5 (Cloth)

Printed in the United States of America

Preface

"What more can I do?"

The tests are marked. The scores are low. The question is asked in frustration and despair. It is asked by almost all teachers (and by many parents), and it is asked most often by the most competent, those teachers who have prepared their work in detail, planned their lessons thoroughly, and worked hard with their classes. What more can they do?

This book is an answer to that question. It describes how with limited classroom resources it is possible for children to master basic skills and much more, and for them and their teachers to have a good time doing it.

This is not a book of recipes, nor does it attempt to examine principles or theory. It's a book about what works. It is not the purpose of this book to condemn present methods, or teachers, or children, but simply to examine what it is that teachers are trying to teach and students are trying to learn, and to help them both do their parts more effectively.

The job of teachers is to maximize the possibilities for learning,

v

for children and for themselves. This involves change. And by change we do not mean substitution. It is not especially helpful to replace one set of reading books by another set of reading books, nor to disguise, momentarily, the content of courses by rewriting the titles.

Change necessitates new kinds of attitudes, values, and behavior. This is what teachers are always wanting for children, but they are for the most part unable to attain this simply because their own attitudes, values, and behavior stay the same. It is possible that teachers formerly functioned well as catalysts, but the elements of our society are now so different that the role of the teacher has itself to change.

This book is for parents, too. Admittedly it is written from a teacher's viewpoint, but it is not the conventional viewpoint. Parents, of young children especially, are becoming increasingly involved in classroom work, and understandably they feel a need to emulate the professional approach. Since it is precisely this approach that is found detrimental to learning, it will be an encouragement to parents to participate in activities with children using their unique talents in their own way without the pretense of playing "teacher." Moreover, and in the long run more importantly, if parents come to understand how teachers themselves need to be encouraged to abandon the conventional teacher role, then new possibilities for parent and community relationships with schools will emerge. Mutual help will come to replace mutual recrimination.

What is written is based on observation and experience with children and teachers, in the classroom and outside of it. The emphasis is on action, on how to go forward, and how to keep on going.

Coventry, Connecticut ANNE BREMER
January 1972 JOHN BREMER

Contents

CHAPTER ONE

Classroom Conversation

"What More Can I Do?"

This is the question teachers ask. There is no shortage of answers. There must be more discipline, more books, more money, more materials, more schools. Lessons must be better prepared. Teachers must be better prepared. There are vast quantities of information available to help them. There are pamphlets, magazines, articles, guides, all manner of secondary expertise. There is research and counterresearch. But teachers still ask. Their question is not answered. They are told what can be done, but that is very different from what they can do.

In this they are like the children who cannot read. All sorts of help is given, but the children still say, "I can't." And really this is not too much different from the young child who cannot walk. He has to take the first step. There is no other way. When he can walk he can be helped to walk better, further, faster, but the walking is his skill alone. So too a child must read the first word, and when he can read he can be helped to read even better. So too a teacher must learn to teach, and the action of teaching has to be the teacher's alone. The help that teachers presently get is an appendage to their experience, and as such cannot really help. It is like giving the toddler a new pair of shoes to help him to walk, or a dictionary to help the child learning to read. (As a matter of fact, this is often done.) Essentially for help to be useful it has to be self-help based on that first step, based on what is already known and experienced. To answer the question, "What more can I do?" the "I" has to "do" something. That something has to be a part already of the "I." What is done will be done because intuitively it is felt to be appropriate, to be the next step, the next learning action.

In order to help teachers answer their own question in their own way it is necessary to help them see what it is they are already doing, what it is they already know, and what it is they suspect. It is this suspicion that has to be nurtured. It is this suspicion which borders between knowledge and ignorance that is the starting point of learning. It is at that point that we shall find the clues for new action.

Our search for clues begins with observation. Let us look at some classroom situations.

It is third grade reading time:

TEACHER: Find page 32. Who can tell me the title of our new story?

CHILD A: "The Friendly Frog."

TEACHER: What do you know about frogs?

CHILD B: They live in ponds.

TEACHER: What is a pond?

CHILD C: Water.

TEACHER: You must answer with a sentence. What kind of water?

CHILD C: Green water.

TEACHER: Yes, but answer with a sentence please. Say some more about the water. What makes it green?

CHILD C: It's just that color.

TEACHER: Yes, but what makes it that color?

The teacher spends the next fifteen minutes trying to get an answer to that question. The class becomes increasingly restless. They don't know the answer. Maybe "The Friendly Frog" would tell them, but they don't have time to read the story now.

As we observed this situation we found ourselves at first somewhat in the position of the third grade students, hoping the story might be interesting. Like them we searched in our minds for knowledge of frogs. We felt responsive to the teacher. It was an orderly class, quiet and thoughtful, and the students were prepared to work; we became part of it. But then we got stuck at "green water," and like the students we got exasperated. Tell us if you want us to know. Let's get on with the story. Then, like them, we got bored, and like them we found our attention wandering. It found new focus on the teacher's exasperation. The students had begun to bait the teacher. She had now become the subject of the lesson. In this situation our sympathies changed. Obviously it had become terribly important to the teacher to teach, to get across to the children "her point." The lesson had begun with the children willing to learn. It ended with the teacher desperate to teach. In the situation there was no coincidence of aims and no communication between student and teacher. There were words, there was talk, but there was no conversation.

Let us look again briefly at what happened. The teacher entered the classroom prepared. She knew exactly what she was going to do and what it was she wanted of the students. The students too had expectations of their teacher. They knew the pattern. They knew that to succeed they needed to perform a ritual, to follow the lead of the teacher, to respond upon request. And since this class had some respect for the teacher, no matter for what reason, they were willing to succeed. But it appears that willingness of students and willingness of teacher is not a formula that necessarily leads to learning. We see indeed that willingness to teach may lead to the destruction of willingness to learn.

The teaching consisted of asking questions. The children were subjected to a search. It was as if first they were the subject of the lesson and then, as we said before, that the teacher was the subject. The planned material of the lesson was never the subject.

It can and should be argued that the teacher was insensitive to the needs of the class, that she ought by experience to have known that her line of questioning was not profitable to the course of the lesson, that she in effect departed from her lesson plan. Let us give this teacher, then, the benefit of inexperience. The children could not answer her questions. Let us see now what happens when they can.

It is time for fourth grade science:

TEACHER: What did I do?

CHILD A: You dropped a piece of chalk.

TEACHER: What happened to it?

CHILD B: It broke. (*Muffled laughter*)

TEACHER: What else happened? (*Pause*)

TEACHER: Which way did it drop?

CHILD C: Sideways.

TEACHER: Sideways! How do you mean?

CHILD C: Well, it fell sideways, not point down.

TEACHER: Yes. You say it fell?

CHILD C: Yes.

TEACHER: So, what happened to it?

CHILD C: It broke.

TEACHER: No, I don't mean that. What happened immediately after I let it go?

CHILD D: It fell on the floor.

TEACHER: Good. "It fell." Why did it fall?

CHILD E: Because you dropped it.

TEACHER: But it didn't fall upwards did it?

CHORUS: No.

TEACHER: Why not?

CHILD F: Because it is heavier than air.

TEACHER: Yes. What other reason?

CHILD F: Because air is lighter than it.

TEACHER: Yes. Look, what makes things fall?

CHILD F: Because of the earth's gravitational pull.

TEACHER: Good. You know all about it. Are there some things heavier than air that don't fall down?

CHILD F: Airplanes.

TEACHER: I didn't mean airplanes. Can you think of something else?
CHILD F: Birds.

In this lesson it is clear that a number of children know the answer expected, but they are not about to give it. They exercise their intelligence, first, by playing with the system in perpetuating the initial question, then by playing with the teacher, and finally by playing against her.

The lesson plan begins, as in our first example, with a question and answer session. The pattern of the two situations, the way they turn out in the classroom, exhibits interesting similarities. Again the children are subjected to questions and hence become the subjects investigated; that is, *they* become the subject of the lesson. The willingness of the children to learn is at odds with the willingness of the teacher to teach. It occurs at different places in the lesson. There is, as before, no coincidence of aims. After the initial subjection comes the retaliation, and the teacher becomes, as before, the subject of the lesson. Again we see in the pattern of question and answer no communication, only barriers to it. Ignorance was the effective barrier in our first example, but, strangely, understanding appears as the barrier this time. The children do understand what answer to give, and indeed if we examine the answers "airplanes" and "birds," we see how beautiful and how challenging is the intelligence of these children. These answers contain in them not only the bait to exasperate the teacher, and the literal answer to the question, but also implicitly a question in return, one that probes the mysteries of physical forces other than gravity. It is an appeal to the teacher to teach. We see here children's natural desire for knowledge and their great willingness to learn. These children are displaying over and over again "their needs," as jargon has it. Simply "teach us."

Make no mistake, this teacher is doing her job. She has planned her work according to the method prescribed in her training. The subject is given in the curriculum guide. The problem is that in doing her job, teaching, no satisfactory learning is taking place, nor can it take place. The rigidity of the lesson plan and of the material cramp the intelligence of the children. As soon as the teacher begins to succeed in motivating the children they overrun the boundaries prescribed for them. They exhaust the available classroom resources, particularly the teacher's own knowledge. There is nowhere for them to go, nothing tangible for them to do, nothing to investigate, nothing to come to grips with intellectually or literally. Their recourse is either boredom or, what is more fun, the demoralization of the teacher. Ironically, the more successful the teacher is in motivating the children, the easier it is for the children to divest her of authority.

Now the teacher knows that the children are getting at her, but she persists, nevertheless, for after all, what are the alternatives? To give the answer she has in mind is clearly not "teaching." To follow the leads given by children would take the lesson out of the security of its plan. Also, by taking the initiative of the children the aim of the lesson might not be accomplished, in which case the teaching, according to the conventional criteria, will have failed. But far worse, from the teacher's point of view, she is not qualified in science and most likely has no knowledge beyond the confines of the prescribed curriculum. Not to be an authority gives rise to intense anxiety. Furthermore, no good can come from departing from the original plan if the teacher cannot teach, since, according to current thinking, under these circumstances no learning can take place.

So there the poor teacher is, trapped in the classroom, trapped by ignorance, surrounded by intelligent and hostile children. Again, "What more can I do?" that poor teacher asks.

Suppose, however, that the teacher had succeeded in her objective, that the children had found out, or been told, or somehow acquired a few facts concerning gravity; it is exceedingly unlikely that they would have acquired the skills of investigation, that they would have stumbled upon a problem and learned what a problem is. And in our earlier example of reading it is equally unlikely that had the teacher succeeded in her aims the children would have acquired the arts of language.

Looked at in this way the failure of teachers may well turn out to be the beginning of their success, for heaven help children if their teachers really succeed!

This question-answer technique of teaching predominates in all elementary grades—so much so that it is quite usual for any child in kindergarten through grade six to be asked upwards of 1000 questions a day.

After observing one hour of intensive questioning in a classroom we feel exhausted. We just want to be left alone. Our response is to get up and walk out. The children do not have that option.

Often when our own ignorance is prodded we feel resentful and guilty, and sometimes just plain hurt. It's not our fault we don't know. And sometimes when we know the answers a pattern takes shape, and we want to ask a question or follow a new line of reasoning. But we can't. And sometimes, too, we think the teacher is wrong, but there is no way to say this.

It is hard to know how children feel about this constant attack, for that is what it amounts to. Whatever other feelings it arouses, friendliness is not one of them, and it must perforce be absent for a large part of each day. Any knowledge acquired during this time is thus not associated with friendliness. There can be no love with learning, and no love of learning. Pride there may be, and triumph, but no great virtue. Children are not learning the humanities.

As observers we must be concerned to discover what this technique does achieve.

A question is asked. If the child doesn't know the answer, then he needs to be told. If the child does know the answer, then he doesn't learn more by being asked. Either way, no learning takes place. We have talked about this with a lot of teachers. Invariably their comment is, "Yes, but a class is different from one child. If the child doesn't know, someone in the class does know and will give the answer, thus teaching the child who needs to know." This, of course, is the case. In this situation what role is the teacher playing? It seems to us that she enables students in the class to become teachers of other students. She is a catalyst in the situation, enabling teaching to take place, but not herself teaching. If this is so, the question-answer technique is not a technique of teaching but a means of enabling information to be given. Now there are many other ways in which information can be given, and since in our observations so far we have seen very clearly the destructive aspect of the question-answer technique, we might well begin to question its value in the classroom at all. As to its "enabling" role, we might well ask what kinds of understandings the students involved have. The teacher-student gains glory in the eyes of the teacher. There is pride in success. The enabled student is passive in the situation and may well feel jealous or angry with the teacher-student. There is no way for the enabled student to be actively involved in the learning. There is no process to be gone through, nothing to explore. The enabled student is a picker-up of crumbs, when what is needed is a meal—for everyone.

Let us carry the teachers' argument one stage further. If indeed, as seems to be the case, it is the child who knows the answer who teaches the child who doesn't, the learning takes place between the statement of one child and the silence of the other. If it were possible to find some way in which the learning silent partner could become active and responsive to the knowing child, then the involvement of both would give rise to greater understandings, both of the subject matter and of the social interaction necessary for such understandings. Instead of harboring competitive and antisocial feelings the children would be much more likely to learn the values of cooperation. Information becomes transformed by its use as a cooperative medium into understanding, and the understanding is not just of the information but of and between the participants in its exchange. Clearly, what is missing in the question-answer situation is conversation. It is really not possible for children to talk to one another naturally, nor for the children to talk with the teacher naturally. There are demands and responses, but no give and take.

Let us take just one more example. We shall observe a mathematics lesson. This class is especially good in conventional terms. The room by material standards is in the luxury class. It has wall-to-wall carpeting. It is light and airy and overlooks well-kept lawns. Children are seated in small goups, three or four to a work area. There are eighteen children and two teachers, one of whom is teaching:

TEACHER: Tracey, you come and be our model. Now, Tony, here's the tape. See how tall Tracey is. That's right. Neil, you help him. Hold this end. (*The children work together in front of the class. Everyone watches.*) Now, Tony?

TONY: It's one measure, that's 60 inches, that's 5 feet.

TRACEY: I'm not 5 feet tall.

TONY: Yes, you are.

TEACHER: What do you think, Neil?

NEIL: This is a silly way to do it. The tape goes in and out. You can't hold it straight.

TEACHER: Good. You mean we can't get an accurate measurement this way?

NEIL: Right.

TEACHER: Well, what can we do about it? (*Chorus of ideas from the children*) Hold it. Mark, you seem to have a good idea.

MARK: Well, at home my mother makes me stand against the wall. She puts a book on my head, and then we measure from the book down the wall to the floor.

NEIL: Let's do it.

Mark comes from his desk with a book. Neil pushes Tracey against the wall and takes the tape from Tony, who stands by and looks on. They work together, a small group engrossed in activity.

NEIL: It's 54 and a bit—54½ inches.

TEACHER: Good. So how tall is Tracey?

TONY: She's 4 feet and 6½ inches.

TEACHER: Good. Someone come and check it. Margaret.

We have here an example of teacher and children working in harmony. The teacher responds to suggestions from the children, and they respond to her. The problems are understood by the children, posed by them, and solved by them. There is an excitement in the room. The focus of attention is the measuring, and the aims of the teacher and of the children are coincident, namely, measurement accuracy. We notice that conversation is an integral part of the accuracy. True, the teacher asks questions to shift the emphasis to productive argument, to clarify a point, or genuinely to request a new lead in the activity, but the questions are not disruptive.

What we have observed here occurs in the best conventional settings, not in every lesson but at least two or three times a day for a few minutes each time.

Let us continue the observation. The teacher has put up on the board a rudimentary graph, with height measured on the vertical coordinate and students' names given on the horizontal. Tracey's height is represented by a bar at 4 feet, 6½ inches. Now it is Stephen's turn to be measured by Daphne and Maurice:

TEACHER: Hold the book flat, Maurice.

DAPHNE: The numbers aren't right.

TEACHER: What do you mean?

DAPHNE: Well, it can't be . . .

MAURICE: Turn the tape round, stupid.

DAPHNE: Don't call me . . .

TEACHER: All right, that's enough. Now (*putting the tape right*), how's that?

DAPHNE: That's O.K. It's . . . 57 inches.

TEACHER: So, how tall is Stephen? (*Long pause. Lots of hands go up.*) Hands down. Now, Daphne, let's spread the tape out and you count out the feet. Where is 1 foot?

DAPHNE: Here.

TEACHER: At 12 inches.

DAPHNE: Yes.

During the next three or four minutes Daphne, with the teacher's help, works out the answer. Meanwhile, the other children who have nothing on their desks get restless and talk to one another, quietly though. These remarks are overheard.

At Tony's table:

TONY: Stephen is taller than Tracey.

DORETTA: Well, she's a girl.

TONY: So what?

SUSAN: Boys are just taller than girls.

MICHAEL: Not always. Henry, he's . . .

SUSAN: I mean mostly they are.

TONY: My father is taller than my mother.

MICHAEL: Yeah, so's my uncle.

SUSAN: Well, how about lions and tigers?

TONY: Well, how about lions and tigers?

SUSAN: Well, the male is always bigger. (*Oohs and ahs of general agreement*)

At Mary's table:

MARY: I wish we could go outside.

DEBORAH: So do I. We could play jump rope.

MARY: Let's do that, after school.

DEBORAH: O.K.

STEPHEN: (*Joining the girls*) Girls!

At Larry's table:

LARRY: You know, you could do that with flowers.

KENNY: Do what?

LARRY: Measure them. You could make a chart, you know, and
. . . . Maybe they grow different heights, like people.

KENNY: Course they do.

LARRY: What do you mean? They're different. They're flowers.

KENNY: Yes, but they're alive aren't they?

LARRY: What do you know about it? My father . . .

What we have overheard is talk clearly different from the kind
that took place between teacher and student.

If we look for a moment at Tony's table, we see a group of
children who by their talking together came to an agreement about a
general proposition clearly related to the lesson. Again we see the
magnificent intelligence of children comprehending the universal
principle. The teacher is concerned to teach measurement of length
as well as accuracy in measurement. But the children have learned
in this situation much more. The teacher's problem now is how to
respond in such a way that the learning can be ordered and organized
by the children so that their powers of discovery are not belittled nor
jeopardized and their intelligence not cramped. Again in this situation, from the point of view of teacher success, the question is,
"What more can I do?" Teachers are not superintelligent human
beings. The sum total of the intelligence of the students in the class
is far in excess of that of the individual teacher.

Let us look now at Mary's table. Two children are quite uncon-
cerned with the lesson, and their thoughts are about their own business. Here is conversation which apparently does not lead to learning.
This is true if we are thinking here only of children. But we the
teachers learn something very definite. Two little girls want to play
jump rope. Is it possible that this activity permitted in class time

could lead to the teacher's aim for the lesson? Suppose the two girls were given half a dozen jump ropes each, of different lengths, and were asked to find out which they could best jump with, and to find out why this was so, and to find out whether the relation of height to rope length was the same for the two of them. These problems could be posed, recorded, and developed in a number of different ways, depending largely upon the understandings the children gained as they went about their work and talked, conversed, about it. But it is not hard to see that, for example, linear measurement, ratio, and averages must of necessity be a part of the work task, and most important that they are there because of the natural differences between Mary and Deborah.

At Larry's table, as at Tony's, conversation is directly related to the lesson. It does not lead directly to learning, however, but to speculation, to possibilities for learning. It is precisely this wonderment, this play of intellect, that all teachers want for their students. It is there in the classroom, over and over again, whenever conversation breaks out. In the normal course of events it is curbed and quieted. Sometimes it is overheard by accident, but it is not listened to, nor encouraged, nor given any functional place in the regular classroom. It is not recognized.

Let us continue our observation of this math lesson.

By now the graph on the board has five names on it. The children are good natured but very restless. They are expected to sit and watch as each child has a turn to participate in the measuring activity. At Tony's table the children are impatiently waiting to have their generality verified. Michael can't control himself any longer, and in a loud voice proclaims to the class that on the graph the boys are always taller than the girls.

TEACHER: Yes, Michael. How clever of you to spot that. You're quite right.

MICHAEL: And mothers and fathers . . .

SUSAN: And lions and tigers . . .

TONY: Yes, all things and animals.

MICHAEL: No, not always. (*Great confusion and excitement*)

TEACHER: All right, one at a time, please. Now, Michael, you were saying about mothers and fathers . . .

MICHAEL: Well, fathers are taller than mothers, mostly.

TEACHER: Yes. I see you've been thinking about this. Good. Now, do we have our last measurement up? Yes. That will do for today. Tomorrow we'll do some more measuring and see if we can find out what the average height of the class is.

It is hard to condemn the teacher for this trivial ending. She clearly feels threatened by the violence of expression from Tony's table. She understands that the children have anticipated her teaching, which is a nuisance, because now she is left unsupported by her plan. Her response is to terminate the difficulty and switch to something new. The lesson was in conventional terms a success. The children really thought and learned. We the observers saw that the teacher also restricted that learning and that her success in motivating the children threatened to turn an orderly classroom into chaos. Given the most ideal conditions and a skillful, mature teacher, it was apparently impossible to maximize learning conditions.

As an observer of classroom situations we are left with a number of impressions. First, it appears that good teachers and inexperienced teachers alike, restricted by present teaching conventions, cannot even begin to tap the learning potential of the class. Moreover, it is likely that certain kinds of teaching successes create impossible learning conditions. Second, it seems that teaching, whatever else it is, has something to do with communication, and that communication between teacher and student does not take place effectively by the universal question-answer technique. Third, we note that where there is a lack of communication about the subject matter of the lesson, either the children or the teacher become the subject of the lesson, that is, the focus of attention, and that either way feelings get in the way of learning. Fourth, in the lessons we observed learning took place when the teacher was inactive with respect to most of the students.

These impressions provide us with clues for finding a positive starting point in a new teaching strategy.

At the end of a school day teachers go home tired. Teaching is an exhausing business. Mostly the fatigue is not physical but emotional. Teachers spend an enormous amount of energy trying to keep children quiet.

"Stop talking." "Quiet, please." It is difficult to stop children from talking. Talking is as natural as growing. Teachers do not say "stop growing," but it may be that this is precisely what "stop talking" means. If talking leads to conversation to communication and to learning, if this is a necessary, natural order, then to stop talking is to stop learning, and to stop learning is to stop life. No wonder children fight their teachers. They are fighting to survive.

Intuitively many teachers understand their predicament, but they do not readily see what to do about it. You can't just let children talk, though we don't know why not. But let us take the teacher's point of view. Suppose, then, as many teachers do, that we recognize that children have to talk. Let us provide something for them to talk about that will lead to learning, the aim of the lesson. Most often this means that the teacher provides a picture or an object for the children to look at. This they dutifully do. Comments are desultory, and soon the teacher gets anxious and wants the children to talk, to make connections between things, to be curious and ask questions, and eventually her need is so great that she begins to encourage them. She asks a question. She asks a question about the picture or the object, and pretty soon we are back where we started, at questions and answers. Conversation there is not.

Some teachers plan conversation lessons. In kindergarten a story is read, and thereafter the children act it out in their own words. The teacher has in mind a variety of aims—story recall, improvement of diction and speech patterns, learning of vocabulary, enjoyment of drama, and so on. At all grade levels there are variations on this theme. In addition, with older children citizenship and democratic procedures are practiced conversationally. There are debates and elections. There are discussions and committees. When observed closely, however, these lessons have in them little of true conversation. It is true that conversation is not seen for the most part as a direct aim of the activity, but where it is, and for the moment this is our interest, the lesson is understood as a device to encourage conversation. This is the way the teacher thinks of it.

As observers we see that the device in operation becomes a way of manipulating children's conversation, and when conversation is manipulated, that is, controlled, by a third party, a teacher, it becomes not conversation but debate, not exchange but at best statements of opposition and caricatures of opinion.

Simply to see a lesson plan, the intent of which is to encourage conversation, must make us pause. It surely takes a special kind of person to imagine that conversation is something that needs encouragement. Conversation is natural. Why then the need to encourage it? If conversation is a basic human skill, what need for a lesson? Skills need to be practiced, but it appears as though lessons, as commonly devised, are inappropriate means for even producing conversation, much less for practicing it. We therefore come to an interesting conclusion. If conversation is vital to learning, and if it cannot take place in the conventionally structured lesson, it would seem that lessons and learning do not go together.

"The tests are marked. The scores are low." Most teachers already suspect that lessons and learning do not happily go together. As observers we can begin to see why they don't.

Suppose now we use our prime clue and take conversation to be the starting point of our learning, and suppose, too, that we recognize our need to learn first what, as teachers, we must do, then we have a method, and we have a direction of inquiry.

Let us pursue our inquiry.

CHAPTER TWO

Lunchroom Talk

"What More Can I Do?"

Miss Smith, sandwich in one hand, pencil in the other, is working her way through a mass of papers:

MISS SMITH: It's ridiculous! What a waste! We've spent all week on these spellings and they still don't know them. And they're so easy. They should have done these a year ago.

MISS MINELLI: I know just how you feel. (*Sympathetic nods from faculty colleagues*)

As Miss Smith says, "It's ridiculous." But what is it that is "ridiculous"? a wasted week, wasted effort, wasted talent, wasted words?

Miss Smith will not give up, though, nor will her colleagues. Next week it will be the same—and the week after and the week after.

that. There is the conviction that some time the children ought to get their lessons right. It is in this conviction that we begin to see something which sets school life apart from the life outside.

No parent expects that in one or two weeks, or in one or two months, a child will be able to drink from a cup without a spill, but parents never doubt that children will drink. No parent expects that a child will hold a pencil properly the first time, the tenth time, or the hundredth time, yet no parent doubts that the child will make marks on the paper, that he will, in fact, draw. Until a child reaches school age there is little doubt in anyone's mind that he will learn what is required of him; but once a child is in school, teachers, and parents too, begin to doubt, and eventually so also does the child. The teacher is convinced that the child *ought* to be able to do this or that, not that he *will* do it.

Anxiety goes along with doubt, and so, every so often, to assuage the anxiety of teachers and of parents, tests are given, hopefully to show that progress is being made. Judgments are made about children, not to help children learn but to help teachers in their conviction of what ought to be happening. Yet, ironically, most tests seem to render teachers more anxious and more doubtful than ever.

Let us go back to Miss Smith. She recognizes that something in the pattern of teaching and testing spellings is a waste. But the commitment to continue the pattern is clearly as strong as ever. Her remark that the spellings were "so easy" gives us perhaps another clue in our search for needs and new action. This is work that should already have been covered, that should already be known by the students. This belief is common among all grade teachers, from kindergarten up.

"They (the children) don't know their colors yet, so we can't play that game."

"They simply have no concept of up and down, so I can't use that method for teaching them to make their letters."

"They can't multiply properly, so it will be impossible for them to do areas."

Let us suppose that these judgments about children's ignorance are warranted, which is frequently not the case, it seems to us that the teacher should feel quite happy in this knowledge, because now there is a place from which to begin to teach. The teacher knows the unknown area which tests purport to show. Why not, then, play the game in order to learn the names of the colors? Why not teach the up and down of letters to teach the up and down concept? Why not teach the concept of area to learn the need and skill to multiply? Because the convention of teaching demands that what is taught be simplified, separated into component parts. What happens is that the components fall apart and there is no way then of seeing their relatedness. There is no reason to pick up the pieces, no reason to learn. It is a remarkable child who learns the name of the color blue without first attaching it to something of that color. It is an even more remarkable child who can learn the meaning of "up" without observing something that is up. Outside the classroom we understand this principle quite easily, but back in the classroom children must be taught to multiply before they are allowed to understand why multiplication is necessary.

In the home the principle that children learn by doing is so basic that no one bothers about it. Children learn to walk, to run, to talk, to draw—not because they learn to take one step, then another, then a third, and then how to connect the separate steps. They just do it, and really it does not matter how. In life outside school children do not learn easy things and then hard things. Is not the first step harder than the rest? They learn. They do not learn one thing, then another thing, then another thing. They learn, and when they have learned they are able to communicate that there is this thing, that thing, and another thing.

When one has learned the logic is easy, the steps are simple. The learning consists in discovering the pattern. When it is seen the learning has taken place. So, in school we give easy spellings, graded on a level. Maybe it is precisely because the words are all on the same level that they are so difficult to learn. They are too much the same, and it takes a superintelligence and a superperception to work out the distinctions in order to learn the easy spellings.

Teachers are sometimes surprised by the child who spells "hippopotamus" when he finds "cat" too difficult. But every parent knows with joy that his child can and does do his special thing. Parents know the natural. Teachers are surprised by it.

Teachers are surprised, too, by how destructive children are. But it is teachers who make destruction a necessary part of children's learning.

When material logically ordered is given to children there is no pattern for them to discover. It is presented to them. If they see it, then they already know the material. If they don't see the pattern, that is, if they need to learn, they will have to work with the material —manipulate it, change it, in a word, destroy what is given—before they can begin to discover the pattern. But destruction is not allowed. Destruction is penalized. Hence so is learning.

There is a set of conventional rules for how to plan a lesson, and teachers every week write their lesson plans. There is also a set of conventional ways of thinking about the results which stem from these lessons. It is clear that the conventions come to be considered natural by many teachers. They are convinced of what children ought to achieve, and they are certain that a progression in steps from easy to hard will eventually enable them to achieve. Teachers see their problem as one of simplification, that is, of breaking the subject to be learned into smaller and smaller fragments. But all children know that the whole cake is much more attractive than a small bite!

Miss Smith has marked the papers. She has done her work. She has done the best she can, but she is not very happy. She really is concerned about the children. Surely they can't be as stupid as all that. Miss Smith's natural feelings about children are getting the better of her professional attitudes.

"If only there was something more I could do."

So often in the field of education we hear about the needs of students, but here we can sincerely sympathize with the needs of teachers. They, like their students, know there has to be some other way. Out of this very expression of need we begin to see that other way. Miss Smith is expressing *her* feelings, not the conventional feelings. She is expressing *her* natural anxiety. She is for a moment an individual.

"What can *I* do?"

Here we have it, the beginning of an answer. If in her relation with the children Miss Smith could find her natural self, if she could be that "I," if she could individualize her teaching, then the conventional pattern would be broken. When that happens Miss Smith would be operating on her natural belief that children are not as stupid as all that. And when Miss Smith operates on this belief she will discover just how intelligent children really are, and how well they can perform. Strangely enough, Miss Smith, in her professional training, will probably have been taught this very principle, that to believe someone to be intelligent produces intelligent behavior from them, together with the experimental proof. Ironically, she has been taught, but she will not have learned, until now, through her experience.

There are many Miss Smiths. And there are many expressions of need. Let us continue our observations in the lunchroom:

MR. BROWN: That Kenny! One of these days I'll kill him.

MRS. COHEN: What has he done now?

MR. BROWN: Just tore his book up.

MRS. COHEN: How come?

MR. BROWN: That's just it. I don't know. He's been working a lot better lately, untidy still, but better. And I went over to see how he was doing. They were writing a story, you know. I just suggested he try to keep the words touching the margin, and he jumped up in a great huff, tore his book in half, and threw it at me. Really, what can you do with a boy like that?

MRS. COHEN: What did you do?

MR. BROWN: I told him to pick it up.

MRS. COHEN: Did he?

MR. BROWN: Not likely. Just stood there and swore at me. Well, I couldn't let that start again. I sent him to the office.

MRS. COHEN: Did he go?

MR. BROWN: Yes, fortunately.

Mr. Brown is upset and he is puzzled. His relation with Kenny has obviously been improving of late and now, for apparently no reason, comes Kenny's outburst. At this point it would be usual to try to find the reasons for Kenny's outburst, whether it was provoked by Mr. Brown, and what Mr. Brown ought to have done. Let us suppose that the reasons could be discovered, it is very doubtful that they would really help Mr. Brown or Kenny. Instances are specific, and while perhaps over a period of time patterns of behavior are seen to emerge, nevertheless, the instance is unique, and it is precisely this with which Mr. Brown, and all teachers, have to cope. Reasons come in retrospect. They are not part of the happening as and when it occurs. So let us not try to probe and analyze the history of this incident, but take it as it is, and see where it is appropriate to go next. Mr. Brown seems indeed to have reacted in this way. Kenny tore his book, so now he must pick up the pieces. But this Kenny cannot do. Something for Kenny has been destroyed, and the literal pieces cannot be picked up until something inside Kenny can be reconstructed too. Thus there comes a point when Mr. Brown cannot go further in his relation with Kenny, and at that point he has to send Kenny away. It is precisely at that point that learning has to take place. It is the point at which Kenny has arrived, and he must be helped to go further. But there is apparently no conventional way Mr. Brown can give him that help. The point at which the student needs the teacher most is the point at which the teacher is least able to help. This situation, then, is not in principle different from our previous examples. That is, when the teacher has learned the point at which knowledge ceases and ignorance begins, he has no effective place to go, but must retreat to what is already known. "They can't multiply so it will be impossible for them to do areas."

It begins to look as though the teacher is in a constant state of retreat. If indeed this is so even for only a part of the time, it is inevitable that children come to know it and that they in their turn retreat also, getting further and further away from the conventional educational goals. Both teacher and student are failing.

Toward the end of his conversation Mr. Brown's feelings have abated somewhat. He got rid of Kenny, and of his anger. This for Mr. Brown is fortunate, and in the conventional class fortunate for the other students too, since Kenny is clearly a disruption.

From Mr. Brown's comment, "I couldn't let all that start again," we can reasonably assume a pattern of behavior which has as its automatic consequence the sending out of Kenny. He is sent because he is disrupting the class, because he is setting a bad example, swearing, and because Mr. Brown wants to make of him an example to the rest of the class: This is what will happen to you if you misbehave. Mr. Brown does not seem to suffer, as some teachers do, from a sense of guilt in having to send Kenny because he himself can't cope. It is a perfectly straightforward, ordinary thing to do, and Mr. Brown does it. Because it is just this we can now begin to understand what a serious difficulty we have uncovered.

The essence of a habit is its sameness and its resistance to change, for to change means to break the habit. Whatever else learning may be, its essence is change. When someone has learned something they have learned it because they have changed their behavior, their way of doing something, their way of thinking. Thus when a pattern of behavior becomes established in which, as in Kenny's case, the end product is automatic, then no learning is possible on the part of any of the participants.

If we enlarge this instance a stage further and think of the teacher playing a conventional role in not one but in many circumstances, and if we recognize that children too are playing a conventional role, then the habits of school life are the antithesis of learning.

When children fail in their roles, when they create disorder amid the school's order, when they perform outside the boundaries of habit, whether these performances are intellectual or social, they cause trouble, and teachers reject them; and yet it is because they cause trouble, and when they cause trouble, that children are potentially the most successful learners. They have survived habit and are fighting to live and to lead.

If we wish to be concerned with learning and creating ways of helping children to do what is natural to live, we as teachers might well begin to look at precisely those problems which arise in the classroom where action and interaction presently cease.

Mr. Brown's concern was to get rid of Kenny, for the sake of the class, but perhaps we ought to be concerned to keep Kenny for the sake of the class, even perhaps for the sake of Mr. Brown.

Teachers who feel that to send a child to the office reflects on their integrity as teachers are in as difficult an educational position as Mr. Brown. Their reason for sending or not sending a child has nothing to do with helping the child. Until the reason behind what is or is not done is to help the child, neither the child, nor the teacher, nor the class, nor the school can learn from the experience.

We see then that comments by faculty about the bad work and the bad behavior of children reveal a set of conventional attitudes. It is these attitudes that are damaging to teachers as individuals. Where are their individual attitudes? How do they really feel? Maybe this is what teachers have to find out.

From a child's point of view the teacher's attitudes are known, because they are conventions. They can be made fun of. They can be feared. But there is no way for a child's reactions to become inter-actions. No personal relations are possible. There is nothing to grow with. Even when the façade of a teacher is broken through by genuine personal feelings, these feelings are generally hostile and it is hard for two-way communication to take place. Spontaneous affection from teachers is rare. It is also suspect. Children know the rules, the conventions, and any departure from them is either "wrong" or a "trick." Teachers do not behave in that way.

Teachers do not have alternatives, then. There is nowhere for them to go. Conventional boundaries limit their growth just as they limit their students. We might conclude from this that the way to teach is to avoid being a teacher.

In a way most teachers know this already. The best-loved teachers are those who are most human, that is, those who are least like teachers, those who have preserved to a large extent their individuality.

Before we leave Mr. Brown's story there is one more aspect of it we should consider, namely, sending Kenny to the office.

In Mr. Brown's action of sending Kenny to the office we see an expression of need, the need for someone else, someone impartial, to deal with Kenny. We can sympathize with Mr. Brown. He has his problems and his anger to deal with. He needs help. He needs support. In this he is like Kenny. The problem is that the office is very likely neither a friend nor a support either to Mr. Brown or to Kenny. It is a higher authority, and authorities make judgments. The higher the authority, the greater the misdeed becomes. What started out as a flash of temper may become magnified to a crime against the dignity of man—or of teachers. This judgment and its assumed impartiality and objectiveness fossilizes the deed. It becomes devoid of associated feelings, isolated from its source, out of context. There it is. And what can Kenny do with it? He can feel guilty, perhaps, or shameful or embittered, but can he learn from his experience? And can he learn from the judgment?

Judgment, whether of spellings or of behavior, is a necessary part of teaching convention for teachers, yet our concern as teachers is how to help students to learn. Testing and judging not only do not help, they obstruct the primary task of teaching.

Our observations thus far in the lunchroom have concerned teachers operating within the teacher conventions, but many express a desire to operate in other ways. Let us take a common example:

MRS. REED: You know, I was thinking how nice it would be to take the children out this afternoon. I'd really enjoy being out in the sun.

MISS JOYCE: Me too. If only we could just go.

Here is a direct and simple expression of desire. Mrs. Reed's comment is that she would enjoy the experience. Teachers plan their activities with the conventionally recognized needs of children in mind. Conventionally there is no recognition of what the teacher enjoys. This situation contrasts oddly with life outside of school where activities involving young children most often devolve upon the group of which they are part. All the participants are active, albeit in different ways.

Mother goes out and the children go with her. She does what she wants to do. She may do it because of some family need, to buy food, or simply because it's a nice day. The children learn from her how to travel in the city, make purchases, do what mothers do. This is very different from the teacher's going out. She may not do things because she wants to. Spontaneity is a luxury not allowed teachers. Mrs. Reed's wishes cannot possibly lead to learning on the part of the children. Mrs. Reed has nothing planned. So goes the conventional thinking. But surely it is precisely because the activity is spontaneous and unplanned that it could lead to learning. Mrs. Reed is feeling warm. Her disposition is sunny. It would be very hard for the children with her not to feel that way too. In such a friendly atmosphere almost any conversation could and would develop into a learning situation. Children's expressions about the sun, its warmth, their friendliness are poetry in the making. The dampness of the soil that simply has to be touched because it is there, the dryness and the roughness of the wall, the heat bouncing off the sidewalk, the sight of garbage or of trees—to the intelligence these things are the raw materials of talk about life and death and growth and decay, about the verities of the planet earth and the mysteries of cosmic speculation.

Too hard for children? Listen to these children overheard in the school yard:

TONY (grade 2): Look what I've found. (*Holds up a crumbled mass of lichen*)

RICHARD (grade 1): What is it?

TONY:	Moon food.
BEN (grade 2):	Where'd you get it?
TONY:	Off the wall. Here.
BEN:	I want some.
CHORUS:	Me too.
ROBERT (grade 3):	Looks like some bird did something. (*Richard pretends to be a bird, flapping his arms.*)
BEN:	You'll make your arms dizzy.
ROBERT:	Arms don't get dizzy.
TONY:	I wonder if birds get dizzy.
RICHARD:	That's silly.
TONY:	You get dizzy when you go round.

It is unlikely that Mrs. Reed would have anticipated this kind of conversation or that she would have been able to do anything about it when it occurred. Children are all the time—in their free time, that is—talking and speculating, as in our example above, but it takes skill to utilize the richness and the variety of children's wonderment to lead them to discovery and knowledge. Mrs. Reed has had no way to learn these skills. She may not go outside.

The teaching conventions rob teachers of their genuine feelings, deprive them of the gratification of personal desires, inhibit their learning about children, and forbid individuality. With their virtues taken away they have no virtuosity. When they are thus professional they are hopelessly inadequate as teachers.

The most common need, and incidentally the one most commonly met, at least in part, is expressed as follows:

MISS BENNY:	This is a very good book. The children are really interested in it. If only we had a few more like it.
MR. CHAPMAN:	You talk about books. What I'd like is some of that new math equipment. Two packets of rods for a whole class. The kids need one each.

Of course Miss Benny needs more books. Of course Mr. Chapman needs more equipment. There can be very few teachers who feel they have all they need. Let us assume for a moment that we give Miss Benny and Mr. Chapman what they have asked for. Instead of ten copies of the book there are now fifty, and instead of two packets of rods there are now thirty. In each case there is simply more of the same. For a while there is excitement in the classes. Then interest in the book dies, and when everyone has rods they lose their attractiveness. They become ordinary. It is true that in most classrooms there is not enough equipment. It is also true that children can have too much of one thing, however good it is.

If we look more carefully at the statements of Miss Benny and Mr. Chapman, we see that more books and more rods are wanted by the teachers. They want them for the children, of course, but the implication is that the teachers want these things to make the job of teaching easier. Suppose the teaching is made easier. What is much in doubt is whether more learning takes place.

When there were only a few books these seemed to the children very interesting. When there were only two sets of rods they were a prize to be competed for. Miss Benny and Mr. Chapman used the materials in the class and by necessity work with them was individualized. The books and the rods were good in comparison with the other available resources. The comparison was made by the children as well as by the teachers. The children were able to use judgment about what they wanted to work with. When everyone has the same materials the work ceases in large measure to be individualized. There are no comparisons possible. Children are no longer able to be the judge of what they want to work with; they become again subservient to the authority of the teacher, however good that authority may be.

Many teachers would probably take issue with this line of argument and claim that the novelty of the materials was what attracted children, and that when this had worn off then of course interest faded. They would be quite right. This is exactly what happens. What Miss Benny and Mr. Chapman do, in fact, is to make quite sure that the novelty wears off by providing everyone with the same materials. Clearly it is an advantage to preserve novelty, to capitalize upon it. Miss Benny does need more books. An assortment of different books would preserve novelty and make it possible, indeed necessary, for children to exercise judgment, a basic skill normally excluded from the school curriculum. Mr. Chapman does indeed need more rods, or at least more manipulative materials, to aid mathematical understanding. Some pots of paint and lengths of dowel rod are all that the class needs to manufacture their own. In the actual making of the materials the mathematical understandings can have a beginning. It is safe to say only a beginning, for once the activity is underway children inevitably make suppositions, see alternative methods of construction, and discover the possibilities of using other materials and other forms. Once children become active it is not possible to stop them from thinking and creating. This probably holds true for teachers too!

Let us make one more observation in the lunchroom:

MISS PETERS: Lesson plans! How I hate that job.

MRS. GROVER: Oh, I don't know. I find them quite useful. I like to know what I'm doing.

MISS PETERS: Yes, but it's all so dull: 9–10 arithmetic; 10–11 reading—every day. No wonder the kids hate it. I hate it.

MRS. GROVER: But you can do different things every day.

MISS PETERS: They look different in the plan, but they're not, really. And the kids know it. And the principal knows it. Everyone knows it. I'm just fed up. If only we could do art at 9 one morning, just for a change.

MRS. GROVER: No. It's good for kids to know what the schedule is. No fuss and bother. We all know where we are.

MISS PETERS: Oh sure! In a great big rut . . .

MR. PATTERSON: Take it easy, Doris. There's not much you can do about it and . . .

MISS PETERS: I'd like to vote them all out of office.

The one thing Miss Peters cannot do is "vote them all out of office." The remark is pertinent, though, since it reveals the pressures of the hierarchy which weigh upon teachers and which they unburden on their students.

Miss Peters' outburst is triggered by the irksomeness of routine and of filling out forms. Mrs. Grover expresses the conventional objective, administrative security. Miss Peters sees this as an interference and not as an aid in her job of teaching. From trivia she turns her attack on the system, wherein is invested the total power; if it is to help her to teach, the system must be changed. But it cannot be changed democratically. It is not democratic. Miss Peters seems to recognize implicitly that the social structure, with its chains of command passed down through successive layers of lesser beings, is somehow at odds with teaching and with learning. The problem is that commands are a one-way thing. Commands necessitate obedience. Obedience given automatically, unthinkingly, is clearly better than that given grudgingly, partially, and with contrary thought. An obedient student is a student only of obedience.

A well-planned lesson does not make a good lesson. A well-ordered classroom does not make a well-ordered class. A badly planned lesson does not make a good lesson either, nor a badly ordered classroom an orderly class. The relation between teaching and learning is not to be found in administrative techniques. Unfortunately, classes, schools, and school systems are operated for the most part as administrative exercises, carried out with more or less efficiency. The criterion of a good class or a good school or a good system is the efficiency of its administration. And as Mr. Patterson says, "There's not much you [the teacher] can do about it."

When you are a small part of the system it's hard to change the whole, but it is not for nothing that we have been an observer of conversations of children and of teachers. From these conversations we have picked up a number of clues which will help Miss Peters to return to her class with a sense that there is hope, that there are things she can do.

Before we go into the class to do some of these things one more point needs to be made concerning our observation of conversations.

There is in the conversations of children and of teachers a rather strange distinction. When children in school are permitted to talk, much of what they have to say about their activities is exploratory and latently, if not actually, productive. When teachers speak of their activities in school there is recognition, mostly implicit, but often directly expressed, of the uselessness of what they do. Hence the conversation usually circles a sore point and functions as a way of bringing temporary comfort through the sharing of anxieties, the airing of anger, and the enlistment of the sympathy of fellow-sufferers. It is perhaps because teachers recognize that somehow their own conversations are nonproductive that they assume children's to be likewise, just chatter. It therefore takes a considerable commitment on the part of a teacher to make an effort to listen to children.

Teachers, of course, know that listening is a skill. They try to teach this skill by having the children listen to them, and sometimes to one another, on command. But the idea that *they* should be listeners—although this is one of the prime activities of a teacher—from the conventional view strikes them as absurd.

Partly because the idea might seem absurd, we have spent this first part of our search for "what to do" doing just that, listening to and thinking about conversation.

CHAPTER THREE

Building Bridges

We have so far in our investigation uncovered a number of possible clues to help us answer our question, "What more can I do?" We have seen that children want to learn and will learn in spite of the teacher. We have seen, too, that teachers want to teach and do teach in spite of the children. Our question has two sides, and our problem is to find a way in which we can bring those sides together to be mutually beneficial.

Clearly, it is not the task of children to initiate this move. The initiative for change lies firmly with the teacher. The teacher must become the prime mover of some new form of educational practice, and the teacher's first task is to learn. In other words, there has to be what looks like a reversal of roles for the teacher. The teacher has to become a student. But a student of what? Since we are looking for new forms, it is unlikely that we can give an answer to that question, at least not yet, since the "what" is precisely what we have to learn. The teacher, then, is a student of what in conventional terms is both the curriculum and the method of its study. In our new terms they are one and the same study, to which we yet can put no name. Now even if logically this is acceptable, practically the situation looks unpromising. How can a teacher put herself in the position, first, of being a student and, second, of being a student of some subject which defies definition and presumably has no authority? The project looks more like a genuine research undertaking than a practical plan for classroom management. This undertaking is indeed very properly research, but of a kind not now in fashion.

Keeping to the simplest form, let us proceed. There are two sides, the teacher and the children, and we will assume, as we did in our old convention, that there is a body of knowledge to be transmitted from the teacher to the children. We have seen that the conventional methods for transmitting the knowledge are largely ineffectual, so what we are searching for is a new means of communication.

For a long time now this problem has been fairly well understood, and a lot of answers have been proposed. Understandably, then, just another answer, however promising, is not likely to be the answer, the panacea, so eagerly sought. What we want is not just another answer but a dynamic, a whole new range of possibilities among which each individual teacher can seek and find his or her own answers.

It is very clear that this elusive means of communication is not to be found within the classroom as it presently is set up, so we must go outside the class, find it, and bring it back.

Let us state the problem again. We have a body of knowledge to be transmitted, and our problem is to find a means of communication. Thus the problem is stated in words. Perhaps there is a solution in words. Play around with language. Play with words. Play. That is what children do. That is the way they learn. Play.

We use language to communicate. Our problem is communication. Language is thus a curriculum and a method. It is for this that we are searching. Play. There is the "other side." We have to reach "them." There is a gap between us—gap in age, a generation gap. There is a gap in experience. There is a gap in race, in religion, in standard of living, in sex. There is a gap simply by virtue of the fact that we are different human beings. Our problem is how to communicate, how to bridge this gap.

Let us translate our problem into something we can come to grips with. Let us bridge that gap.

Suppose the teacher goes into her class, pushes back the desks, and across the floor places end to end some sheets of blue construction paper. This is the barrier to communication. The teacher is on one side, the class on the other. The class wonders what all this is about. They speculate.

"It's a road."
"No, it's for painting. We're going to paint."
"We are going to make a frieze."
"It's a blue line."
"It's for walking on."
"It's a new game."
"It's the Milky Way."

We are teachers. We listen. There is no lack of interest. Most children somehow think of the barrier as though they were on it. It is linear, to be walked on, traveled along. It's a track. They cannot yet cross it. To do so would put them on new territory, on the teacher's ground. It is not a line of communication, but a line parallel to communication. We as teachers begin now more readily to see the power of the hitherto invisible barrier between teacher and student. When an actual barrier is drawn we understand from the conversation how difficult, how unthinkable, is the notion of crossing. So far we have put an actual physical barrier in the place where there is an actual psychological barrier. Now to bridge the gap.

We do not know how to bridge the invisible gap. That is our problem. We are building the bridge to simulate our problem. The materials of which our bridge must be built must be such that they do not readily span the gap. They are too short, too flimsy, and altogether inappropriate for the task. They must stand for our shortcomings, our weakness, and our lack of knowledge. We could carry the metaphor further. Our efforts at communication so far have been many. The failure has come about because they are not of the right kind. The efforts we have made are characteristic of a convention. They may have been many, but they have all been of the same kind. Nevertheless, it is out of these efforts that the new structure has to come. We are what we are. We must grow, that is, learn to be new people. So these materials for bridge building are many, but of the same kind. There are thousands of short lengths, much shorter than the river to be spanned, of flimsy balsa wood (or wooden matches minus their warheads). There are scraps of paper that are too small. There are short lengths of string. There is glue. Nothing more.

We have already put down the "river" in our classroom. Now we put out the materials on our side of the "river," in small piles at intervals along the "river bank."

Speculation continues:

"We're going to make something. Oh good!"
"What is she doing."
"An experiment."

Note here the beginning of a change in responses. There is the sudden joyous "Oh, good!" because "we're going to make something"; alongside is the suspicion that the teacher will do the "doing." But there is something else, too, a sense of mystery. And how appropriate this is. What we do not know is mysterious. To young children everything new is mysterious, something worthy of investigation. Investigation is an adventure. Truly it may demand courage and persistence. In a conventional class all possibility of mystery is destroyed when the lesson begins. The teacher knows her aim. She tells her children, "Today we will. . . ." There is no mystery, no excitement about the unknown, no cosmos. There is no way to practice the basic human skills for adventure, those of courage and of inquiry. Even before we have built our bridge, even before we have begun, even before the task is set, something has happened in the classroom which was not there before, and that something let us call mystery.

"Mystery" is appropriate in another way. We the teachers are searching for an answer. We are involved in a mystery, and suddenly we now have the children involved in the mystery too. When we come to understand this much we the teachers are truly also students. So far, then, our pursuit of a new form has achieved success—not the kind of success that can be measured, evaluated, and graded by some objective authority but a success that we as students know is total. We know unfailingly that we the teachers have suddenly become students in our own classes. We know this. We are our own authorities. We know, as young children know, that they can walk thus far. All this and still without a word to the class about aims and purposes.

Let us consider again the classroom situation. There across the floor is the "river" of blue paper. On one side are the children. On the teacher's side are the materials. The class is still speculating:

"What are all those bits of wood for, Miss?"
"They're like little lamp posts."
"We could make a fence."
"Hey, Miss, can we make something?"
"Yeah, let's make a wagon."

Screeches as of Indian war cries follow.

We have arrived at a point which all teachers fear and which all try to avoid. Many teachers, especially the most able, know that it is not hard to interest children, but they are fearful of stimulating that interest too greatly because there is always a point at which teachers lose control of the situation. The interests of the children come to outweigh the authority of the teacher. However much teachers operating conventionally may recognize the educational values of child-centered activities and the desirability of utilizing children's interests for effective learning, they have not generally been able to find a way of putting their beliefs into practice. The best that can be done is to take children's interests and use them for teaching purposes—that is, the purposes of the teacher, not those of the child, the learner. The best then becomes a seduction of children's activity and creativity. Children are used. Parents, as well as the conventional school administrators, are rightfully angry. Thus we have, at least in part, an explanation of why educational innovation, based on child-centered activity, however attractive it appears in theory, turns out so badly in practice. In a conventional school setting the teacher must be the authority or chaos ensues. So innovation is adapted to fit authoritative necessity and inevitably becomes corrupted. Ironically, the best endeavors turn out to have the worst consequences.

We have in our class reached that critical point which teachers know is to be most feared, the point at which they have to assume control or lose it entirely. If we are on the side of the innovators who advocate child-centered activity, we ought to go with the children. If we are on the side of law and order, we should assume our authority. These are the two alternatives which face teachers. But we are not the teachers in this situation. We are students. This much we have learned. This much we know. We are here to learn more.

Our actions, then, are not reactions. We are not faced with two alternatives but with many possibilities. We are leaders of an activity called learning. And to lead we must learn—now, right now, in front of these other learners.

It is in this moment of stress, of fear, even of panic, that we come to understand most clearly what is the basic skill of teaching, namely, the courage to learn.

Teachers in this position may well cry for help. Theirs is a real cry of need and must be answered.

Earlier we stated that since our means of communication appears not to be within the class, then we must go outside, find it, and bring it back. In moments of stress it is imperative, if we are to maintain our newly acquired status of student, that we behave not as teachers, operating conventionally, but in some other way. Continually, then, we have to search for that other way. Outside of school most likely we would talk over a problem, listen to what other people had to say, and try to understand what was happening. Effectively we would be students. In school we do not need the disguise of teacher. We need simply to be ourselves, students. Emulating our "outside" behavior, we need to listen. We need to look at what is going on, and we need desperately to hear, to understand, and to learn what is being said.

We are in the class, then, trying hard to learn. Over and over again we must face our situation to see what we can understand from it. There is the "river." There are the materials for bridging it. There are the children. What are they saying? Listen.

"What are all those bits of wood for, Miss?"
"They're like little lamp posts."
"We could make a fence."
"Hey, Miss, can we make something?"
"Yeah, let's make a wagon."

Screeches as of Indian war cries follow.

Here is classroom conversation again. What can we learn? First, there is a desire to do something, to "make something." There is here a rapid sequence of development. First there is a recognition of little "bits," then an ordering of these bits into a pattern of "lamp posts" consistent with the linear barrier on the floor, and there is the notion of discrete "bits." Then the gaps between the "bits" are filled in to make a "fence." The pieces are put together with the addition of yet another dimension to the barrier between two territories. And then there is the reiteration of the need to create, and its answer, "a wagon." Creative need is thus expressed in terms of something that will move. Then comes the movement from one territory to another and there is war. Cowboys and Indians can be understood as the metaphor for the battle between students and teacher or students and school authority. Note though that it is a battle that has already taken place. It is historical. The teacher, as we have seen, has a choice either of subduing the enemy and winning the battle or of capitulating. But we are not the teacher, and this is not our metaphor. We are students, and our concern is not to fight for territorial rights and not to live at some past time, but to find the bridge that will allow peaceful, two-way communication between the territories.

Again we see how by operating as a student our thinking changes. Initially we put our problem thus. There are children, there are teachers, and there is, we assumed, a body of knowledge to be communicated by the teachers to the children. Our problem is to find the means to do it. And now, occupied as we are with the metaphor of the bridge, we see that communication need not be unidirectional. We could not have learned this without the children. It is by seeking an understanding of their metaphor, and its link with ours, that the notion of territorial rights has come about, and with it two-way communication between the two territories. The bridge still has to be crossed, however, and we still have to initiate the crossing.

So far in the classroom we have made something to cross, and we have provided materials to make a crossing. We now have to show our willingness to cross in a way that will not be understood as invasion. How does one cross a bridge? Again the answer outside the classroom is obvious. One can walk. One can drive. Suppose we do just that in the classroom.

Take a miniature car. Hold it up. The Indian war cries are silenced. We have entered a new time zone. For the children the metaphor is changing. Take the car and wheel it from the wall at the front of the room to the "river." There it stops, and there the teacher says her first words to the class.

"This car has come to a river. It wants to cross." A short thinking silence follows. In it we too will think about what the teacher has not said.

The teacher did not say:

"I have a car."
"I am driving it."
"I have a problem."
"I cannot cross the river."
"There is no bridge."
"Please build me a bridge," or even, "Please build a bridge."

There is no mention of "I," nor of what to do. Nor does the teacher say:

"How can you get the car across the river?"
"What kinds of bridges could you build?"
"Do you know any bridges like that?"
"How could you fix these materials together?"

There is no mention of "you," nor are there any questions.

Instead there is concentration on the car, in our metaphor the vehicle of communication. The problem must be seen by the children to be solved. Let them come to see it. Do not confront them with it.

The silence is soon broken. Some child will say, "We could build a bridge." All that is left to the teacher at this point is to gesture agreement.

Why only gesture? A personal idiosyncrasy, perhaps, but useful in this way. The teacher in this situation is there to learn, and the relation of learner-in-chief to other learners is different from that of teacher to students. Having arrived at a satisfactory conclusion, from the teacher's point of view, about what to do, it would be so easy for the teacher to say of the students:

"Good."
"Well done."
"Fine."
"Now get to work on it."

All of these kinds of comments imply judgment, and praise, which is what teachers love to give by way of encouragement, but in this instance the teacher is trying to be a student, not in any sense equal with the other students, but a student. The bridge is to be built not in order to please the teacher, not because it is specifically the task set by the teacher (the children were never asked to build a bridge), but because it may provide a means of communication. So far in the activity the children are building a bridge to get the car across the river, to solve a problem. Their activity is not to please the teacher, and it must not be allowed to become so. Many times children will try to make it that, simply because this is the way in which they have been trained in the past, and they still do not recognize that they are there to solve their own problems and to learn themselves. Children do not make it easy for their teachers to learn. Whenever possible, then, in these early learning days for the teacher it is important to say little and do much, to do, in fact, what previously was required of the students.

In the rare event that the children seem unable to cross—that is step over—the "river" to take up the materials, the teacher can take up some materials and step over to the children's side and begin to build her own bridge. Even if the children get themselves started it is often helpful to enter directly into the activity. There is then some evidence for children that the teacher is a student. Moreover, the difficulties which are encountered in the activity, the multiplicity of problems to be seen and solved, the amount of mathematical judgment required, the degree of social cooperation necessary for such a venture, in short, the whole complex of building and learning, are seen and understood from the inside, intimately and personally. Suddenly the teacher, now a student, is working with other students, not working for them, not working to help them, but working with them. The teacher's understandings, perceptions, intuitions, and skills are different from those of the other students, and because they are different others learn more readily. Children will see learning taking place just as they do when father fixes a fuse or mother cooks a new dish.

Let us listen to the conversation around us:

MICHAEL: These bits are too small.

BEN: Stick them together, then.

MICHAEL: Mine keep falling apart.

JOEL: Look at Glen's! How'd he do that?

Building Bridges 39

MARY:	We could use this paper to pave the road.
TANA:	That's a good idea.
BILL:	Here, hold this end.
MONA:	O.K?
BILL:	Yeah, now you do your end.
SUSAN:	I wonder if we can use this (*string*).
VALERIE:	Let's make the George Washington Bridge.
SUSAN:	We want a picture.
DAVE:	What are you making?
BERNIE:	A raft.
DAVE:	A raft?
BERNIE:	Yep. Why not? It's a lot easier than a bridge.
DAVE:	Yeah.
DAVID:	How are we going to keep it up?
JIM:	Put this here.
DAVID:	And this the other side.

The room is full of conversation, genuine interaction, and meaningful exchange. Communications are everywhere—not, it is true, between teacher and student but between student and student. Since we ourselves have become students, we can participate in the communication. If we do this, we further come to understand that what we were looking for as teachers, that is, a means of communication, is now largely irrelevant, since the act of communicating occurs necessarily in association with our other acts of solving the problem of building the bridge or raft. It is not possible to separate the various activities of the class. They are integral parts of one another. Everything is happening all the time. Nor is it possible, while we the teachers continue to be students, for us to be dissociated from the activity of the class and hence from the class. The problem we started with, establishing communication, no longer exists. As many teachers will be quick to see, however, we have not yet solved the problem of transmission of knowledge. In our activity of bridging the gap what knowledge has been gained? This is the great concern of the conventional teacher. From what we have observed so far it would be easy to say, a knowledge of communication. But communication does not happen unless something is being communicated. That something is what conventionally should be transmitted from teacher to child. It should be conventionally a body of knowledge. The conversations so far overheard show children exercising various skills, especially cooperation and an ability to learn from one another. These are clearly basic social skills. They are not, of course, written into any social studies curriculum. At the moment, then, it seems we are at a loss to furnish the conventional requirements. But our lesson has only just begun. Let us see how the activity proceeds.

Gradually groups of children and some individuals fix their constructions in place across the "river." The children are very busy and very talkative, and listening and watching, we become aware of certain general characteristics of the class activity.

First, it appears that everyone is active, even if the activity consists of watching and thinking. Second, the roles which individuals play tend to change quite rapidly. A watcher, for example, will become a speaker and direct a new approach. The leadership of some groups changes with the phases of the work. As children finish their particular contribution, either to a group project or to their own piece of work, they start to wander among the other projects and to criticize and admire methods and achievements. Some children return to their own work to make changes, additions, and improvements. There is no sense of a task too difficult to do. There is no sense of failure, even when a work of art collapses:

MICHAEL: Look out.

BEN: Hold that side up.

MICHAEL: It's going to fall.

It falls. There is laughter from an adjacent group:

MICHAEL: What's so funny?

DAVID: Well, it looked kind of like . . .

JIM: Here. Use this. Put that there . . .

BEN: Gee. That's just what we want.

MICHAEL: How about that!

A real sense of accomplishment, joy, pride, and satisfaction runs through the whole class. Everyone, including the teacher, has done a lot of work, done it well, and had a thoroughly good time doing it.

For the teacher another crucial moment approaches. Time is running out. The lesson must be brought to a close. Some of the bridges are finished. Others look as though they never will be. Some children want to continue. Others have had enough. In the conventional classroom the buzzer sounds and the lesson ends. The arbitrary administrative solution to the problem of concluding a lesson saves the teacher from the dilemma of finding an educational solution to ending it. Normally what happens is that all the materials are put away, including unfinished work, and anything completed is either taken home for the benefit of parents, who then have proof of their children's achievement, or it is commandeered by the teacher for display or other status-making purposes.

We are still working in a conventional school, and shortly the buzzer will sound and the children must be dismissed. Ordinarily there would be a brief review of aims, purposes, and accomplishments. Perhaps all that is needed here is a look at what has been done.

Take up the car again and replay the initiation of activity.

"The car comes to a river."
"It crosses this bridge . . ."

This is a very real kind of evaluation. It is not a judgment passed by the teacher.

The children gather round:

MICHAEL: I bet it won't cross that one.

TONY: I haven't finished mine yet.

TEACHER: It crosses back on the raft.

GARY: Try the ferryboat, Miss.

MARVIN: Can I have a go with it?

CHORUS: Me too . . .

TEACHER: What we need are some more cars.

TONY: I've got some at home. I'll bring them to school tomorrow.

CHORUS: Me too . . .

TEACHER: Then we'd better leave these things right where they are.

DAVID: Can we do some more tomorrow?

TEACHER: Why not?

DAVID: I'd like to make a road . . .

Suddenly the children begin among themselves to talk of new building possibilities. The gap has been bridged.

That was the lesson. Now what? If we look at the results after the children have gone home we see a mighty mess, a lot of bridges, most of them ineffectual, a few rafts stranded and askew, a ferryboat stove in, and a lot of junk. If we evaluate this in our conventional terms, what we do see is a mess, because we are thinking of the finality of the product, of a bridge spanning a river. But if we now look at it in our new way of thinking we are concerned not with an end product but with a continuous activity, communication. What we are in is a workroom, not an art gallery, not a museum. We are in a place where the object is not to get things finished but to keep things moving. We have a direction, but we do not know where we are going. We are headed into the unknown. At the end we are sure of death. We are not looking for an end in the classroom.

As teachers, we are beginning to see an answer to the question, "What more can I do?" In this classroom of a river and bridges the question is much easier to answer, in an immediate way. Obviously we can build better bridges. That much we can see a need for. That much we can do. And children can see the need, and they can do it too. Indeed, they have already gone further and seen the need to link roads to bridges. In our metaphor they are extending the lines of communication.

CHAPTER FOUR

Retrospect and Prospect

You will remember that the bridge-building activity started not because we wanted to teach but because our aim was to learn. And it was our aim, not an aim conceived for the benefit of students. If, then, we take this whole activity and call it a lesson, it is obvious that it has some very unusual features.

Initially we set out knowing that whatever we did was not a part of a curriculum and hence had no claim to a particular subject matter. Our aim, as we have stated it, was to learn, but more specifically, to learn a way of communicating with children. We attempted to do this by building bridges across a visible barrier. Interestingly, the concept of motivation has so far nowhere appeared in our deliberations. To that extent it has been irrelevant, and yet in retrospect we see that the activity of the teacher in placing the materials generated the kind of interest and curiosity in students which it is assumed the motivational procedures of a conventionally planned lesson will produce. Our purpose was not to motivate but to provide a framework, a context, for a task to be performed. It appears, then, that although this lesson was not planned in the generally accepted way, we can in retrospect write for it a plan which enables us to utilize the existing formula. That is, we can use the system for our own purposes. Leaving aside for the moment the first heading, "Curriculum Area," we can go on and make our plan as follows:

Subject: bridge building
Aim: to establish communication between students in the class
(remembering here that we the teachers are also students)
Motivation: layout of classroom
display of materials
Procedures:

1. Introductory activity, by the teacher. The setting of the problem: The teacher takes a car and wheels it to the river. It cannot cross.
2. Main activity, by the students. Bridges, rafts, and other constructions will be built to carry the car across the river, thereby solving the communications problem. During this activity it will be necessary for the students to communicate with one another.
3. Terminating activity: class to view work achieved; evaluation by the teacher. The teacher will take the car to see whether it will cross the bridges satisfactorily.

To complete our plan we now need to consider what curriculum area would be most suitable for our needs. Again, it is our needs as students that we must consider, not the appropriateness of what we have done to an arbitrarily defined body of information. We must use the existing system for our own purposes.

The lesson as described took place just before dismissal. This afforded the teacher a number of advantages, principally allowing time for reflection. The teacher has just been through a tough learning experience and needs a rest. The children have had a similar experience, and they too need a rest period. The intensity of thinking and doing needs a dramatic termination so that the good feelings engendered will not fade by being extended into another school period. The children can go away excited by new prospects. The teacher can sit down and reflect on what this excitement means.

In terms of writing a plan, however, there is a further, practical advantage. We have admitted our inability, indeed our unwillingness, to think of our activity as subject oriented, so that we cannot presume to affix it to the basic-skills curricula. Our lesson, then, cannot be fitted into the morning routine of math and language arts. We have to utilize a part of the schedule which is regarded as less important and relegated to afternoon activities. In practice this time usually turns out to be given to social studies. While there is usually a fairly well-defined format for presenting this subject, there is sufficient latitude for the teacher to insert a lesson which can be conveniently labeled communications, transportation, building developments, architecture (of bridges), or whatever will appropriately fill the given outline. We are well aware of using words to suit our own ends, but in a real sense, since at the moment we have only established a movement of thought in our class, there is indeed the probability that all of the headings we can conceive, and many that we can't, will be covered in some way during our class activity. Retrospectively, we can state precisely the plan of our lesson, and if the school organization (in practice more usually its disorganization) allows us that latitude of planning in retrospect, then we have no problem administratively, that is, with the beginning of our studentship as teachers.

In schools where the class teacher also takes arts and crafts the lesson we have described could be appropriately placed in that category. Here stress would be not on communications, though that is still our purpose, but on structure and form, and our stated aim might be, for example, to explore methods of bridging gaps!

The teacher who has reached this point, who has become seriously committed to learning a new and personal way of teaching and has given some thought to the practical beginnings, even to the details of writing, as we have done, a plan, may feel a sudden surge of confidence. The question, "What more can I do?" is not asked now in a voice of despair, but in a strong and positive way. There is suddenly a new energy released and the teacher begins clearly to see not only that there are all manner of possibilities, but that they can be accomplished, initially anyhow, within the rigid framework of school requirements. The play of words that allows us to bridge gaps has become a play of action too. The existing system can be used.

Feeling as we now do, we are ready to look again at the results of our first experience, the lesson, and to see what more can be done, what more we can do.

Aware that we have not yet begun to communicate a body of knowledge to children—and it is still our assumption, and the conventional assumption, that this is the task of the teacher—we might perhaps begin our thinking about the following activity with this in mind. We might ask what body of knowledge, what kind of information, is appropriate to the task of bridge building. Again we are students. It is fairly certain that we are not, in fact, bridge-builders, and so we need to face the problem in a quite elementary way. Again, too, if we are to find appropriate solutions, we need to go outside the classroom—to go, if only in the mind, to look at a real river and form some idea of the right kind of bridge to build. We find that the real river is not flat like our paper on the classroom floor but is confined between banks, flowing between the mudflats of an estuary or frothing white at the bottom of a ravine. Suddenly we have a new perspective, space.

How did the children think of the river? Let us look at their structure. How wide did they think it was? how deep? how swift? Is it a local river? an imaginary river? one seen on television?

As we look at the structure of various bridges we become aware that we are classifying them. There are some bridges like the George Washington, some like primitive wooden trestles spanning a stream a few yards wide, and some which have used the given materials to solve the problem without seeming to use any specific prior model.

This means, in effect, that we have in our classroom not one river but many rivers, or perhaps one river crossed at intervals along its length from source to tidewater. If, then, we are to continue with our bridge building, it might be well to establish the kind of river our bridge is to span. In our first lesson scale was fixed by the model car, so we could use that as the focus of our next activity. Moreover, the lesson ended with many children wanting to test their structures using the car, and there was also the offer of more cars. This then gives us one set of possibilties.

Let us look again at the bridges the children have built. The

George Washington was built for carrying cars, but what about the trestle bridge? Just before the car was introduced into the lesson the children were operating in a metaphor of historic time, in the time of the Indian wars. The trestle bridge may well belong within that time period even though in the lesson it was supposedly built to carry a car. If we again look carefully at the bridges, we note a number of such anachronisms. It is obvious that individual children have been operating not only within different spatial contexts but also with different time appreciations.

Again we feel a surge of excitement and new-found confidence. We have only just begun, and yet we are finding in our classroom a cosmos. There is time. There is space. There is human experience.

In all this no one has been judged and found wanting.

In our excitement we seem to have departed from our original intention, of finding a way to communicate a body of knowledge. The most we have done so far in practical planning terms is to see the possibility of building a river to put the bridges across! We have been carried away by our own discoveries, and it is easy to think that what we have just learned should become known to the children, that we should explain how some students built their bridges on one set of assumptions and that others focused on a different set. But upon reflection we realize that it was our discovery of the elements of space and time that brought us pleasure, and simply to tell children that this is what they have done would be like telling them "who dunnit." We should be destroying the mystery, and with it the possibility of experiencing what we ourselves have just experienced—the thrill of discovery that makes for love of learning.

We want our students to know what it is we have seen. We feel the urge to communicate. If we look at precisely what it is we are wanting to communicate, we cannot but be struck by the difference between this and what as teachers we were formerly anxious to get across to our students. It seems that what we want to tell them is something about themselves. And again we are impressed by the change that has come over our thinking and our actions. We are not concerned with trying to make school work relevant to to children—relevancy being the fashionable dictum of our time. We have no need to do so. This now is not a problem for us, and we shall not waste our energies trying to come up with solutions.

We do not need to harmonize disparate elements in the curriculum, because we did not start with a breakdown. We do not need a synthesis because there was no analysis. Best of all, we do not need to create relevancy to find meaningful liaison between work task and student. What has been done, and what we understand from it, constitutes a totality.

We do have problems, but they are the kinds which are helpful to our learning and to the learning of our students. There is still the next lesson for both of us.

Our reflections about the first lesson have given us a direction for the second. We want our students to share the sense of joy, of the discovery that they built bridges across a different river at different historic times. There before us is the one "river"—and the mess. Suppose we take out like structures and break up the "river" into a number of parts so that in one corner of the room, near the teacher's desk, for example, we have a piece of "river" and bridges resembling the George Washington. On top of the shelves we place another piece of "river" and all the trestle bridges, and on the window sill we put all that is left. The desks are relocated in their normal positions. Tomorrow we shall operate our class as usual until the last period, and then lesson number two.

At this point we hesitate. Suppose we have been wrong in our time-space discoveries, that what we have thought about the bridges is not really a fact but an assumption. We need not let this kind of doubt deter action. Even supposing we have totally misunderstood and misinterpreted our observations, we shall not communicate in words to children any "facts." We cannot, therefore, feed them misinformation. It is true that we grouped bridges according to our own criteria, but in our instructions for the next activity we shall certainly not insist on maintaining those criteria but rather offer the possibility to children for developing their own.

Can we begin to envisage what is needed as a next activity? Suppose lots of cars are brought to school. What then?

We are now groping again in a confusion of possibilities. We could start with cars, with the width of the river, with the type of brige, possibly even with building a road for the cars. How shall we choose? We could leave the choice to the students. We could simply write a list of possibilities on the board and have them choose a task. We could even get them to suggest what things might be written on the board for them to choose from. There would be nothing wrong with this, except that we are vaguely uneasy about it. This is the conventional method for allowing choice. Somehow it does not seem appropriate for our purposes. As an action it is too well defined. Our purposes are still not yet capable of such clear definition.

Let us look again at that first lesson. There was no instruction to build a bridge, and yet bridges were built. There were materials and there was a problem to be solved. Can we perhaps again provide materials and another problem? What would it be useful to build now?

We began our reflections by going out of the classroom to a river. It was the discovery of the plurality of rivers that triggered our thinking. Could we perhaps provide materials which will enable children to work through some similar experience, working with their hands what we worked in our reflections? Suppose they had some material with which to build a river bank. This would help them to define the kind of river their bridges crossed. But perhaps they would simply line the sides of the strip of blue paper, in effect building another barrier. We need still to emphasize somehow the crossing, the communication, our over-all purpose in this venture. The bridge rests on the banks, but the banks are a part of the land. In our metaphor they bound the information area. This is the area that needs to be developed. It is the information that has to be communicated. We need not confine ourselves to the river and its banks, but we may be concerned with the whole valley. Suppose, then, that we are a little more ambitious and give to the students materials for making land on either side of the river. How would this help? We have already, by splitting up the river, made three major work areas in the room. It is likely that the kind of land built in each of the areas will reflect in part the kinds of bridges in that area, so that we could reasonably assume three different terrains. At least we could assume this if our students had a knowledge of rivers, of valleys, and of bridges that was in some way like our own. Are we then, first, to tell them what our own knowledge is? That is, are we first going to communicate to them information that we already have so that it will enable them to build on our assumptions? Again that vague unease. We sense that such an approach would not be right. It is like the example in our earlier chapter of the teacher who said, "I can't teach areas because they can't multiply." Moreover, we realize that if we do this the children are then going to build on our assumptions, on our fictions. So we hastily abandon that idea, and we are again left with our set of assumptions about what will take place. We cannot really know what will happen. We cannot really plan the next lesson. But isn't our situation now the same as it was in our first lesson? We have to behave as students. We have to find out what will happen. We have to explore the situation as it is happening. We have a beginning. We do not need an end. We have a direction, but we do not know where we are headed.

We have, then, a beginning. At least we can prepare that much. In our first lesson the work area was set up by the teacher and defined by the location of the "river." The specific work areas were set by the placement of materials at work sites. Thus the room was very specifically structured, oriented to the work task. Again we ought to provide quite specific boundaries so that students will know the limits within which they will work.

Again let us consider what we now have. There are three rivers, each with a set of bridges. Our problem is to locate them in the room so that children will understand where they have to work. At the moment the work is portable. After the next lesson it may not be so. What we need, then, is a certain permanence for our work sites. If we are building areas of land, we are going to need space. If there are going to be three different land areas, then we clearly need to find three different permanent work spaces. At this point we are unwilling to alter the conventional classroom structure too greatly, so we have to find ways of creating work surfaces. At the moment the work is linear, but we intend to build areas. There are no spare desks, no tables, nothing. Obviously we need materials to make a work surface. Empty upturned cardboard cartons from the local store, matched in height, stuck together form low portable surfaces, strong enough for our present purposes. Moreover, they have the distinct advantage over regular furniture in that they can only be improved by being worked on with paint and can be papered and plastered and stuck with impedimenta.

What a lot of preparation is needed for our next lesson! Maybe our next lesson should be in furniture-making. Indeed, why not? At this point we are struck by the sudden simplicity of our solution to a lot of the kinds of problems which daily confront teachers: how to get materials, how to make more work space, how to use children's time constructively, especially when they have finished the task in hand, in math or language arts, for example. The teacher doesn't want fast workers to speed on ahead of the class, so would-be workers become bored. The teacher doesn't want to have them get bored, but again the old problem, "What more can I do?" Tomorrow, then, when the quick children have finished their assignments they will be employed sticking boxes together, making work surfaces, preparing for the afternoon's work, our second lesson. How valuable it would be if the children could go get the boxes, that is, work through the whole process, interact with the community, talk to the manager of the store. But perhaps at this stage we feel the energy we would expend in making the appropriate arrangements is too great a demand on us. We do begin to see, though, that suddenly our new way of thinking and of planning impinges upon every aspect of teaching, that the process of preparation and planning suddenly seems now to involve children, and it involves them almost by necessity.

We now have our portable work spaces, three of them, set out with portions of the original "river," crossed by the original bridges. What now? We are still umcomfortably aware that the body of information we are supposed to transmit eludes us. We still want the children to understand something about the differences between rivers, and the different time elements they have been working with, albeit unconsciously. Is this the information we are really trying to convey? The confusion between our assumptions, our understanding, and the facts is the one thing that is clear to us. We need, therefore, to continue to operate as students.

What will the children do? How will they come to know, and what will they come to know? To answer these questions, and to learn, will be the aim of this next lesson, as it was the aim of our first lesson.

CHAPTER FIVE

An Explosion of Learning

Our second lesson is prepared. There are three work areas set out in the class. Each has a strip of blue paper—"a river"— crossed by bridges. Near each work area there are piles of clay or other malleable materials, paper, string, and wood, as in our first lesson. The teacher asks the children to make the land by the side of the river. "Start by your own bridge, ferry, or raft." Work begins. The teacher listens:

TONY: I brought my cars, Miss.

TEACHER: That's useful.

TONY: See?

TEACHER: Yes, I see.

MARVIN: Can I have one?

TONY: O.K., but give it back.

MARVIN: Hey! My bridge works!

TONY: Yeah. It bumps up there.

Together the boys using clay even out the incline and create a ramp. A number of other children are also doing this with the clay.

DAVID: The road comes up here.

JIM: Not like that. It has to be high here.

DAVID: Yeah, but fix this end first.

The teacher has the impression that some bridges are abandoned, that the children are working together on the best bridges, that is, the ones they judge the best, that they are mainly concerned with the logistics of improvement and of tying their constructions to the land.

There are a number of cars, and two boys are playing with one on the floor. Their play is not to be thought a part of the lesson, and the teacher about to intervene observes a boy in a nearby group remonstrate with the players:

BILL: Hey! We need that car. Bring it over.

JOEL: It's ours. You get your own. Here, Jimmy. (*Sends the car along the floor to Jimmy*)

BILL: Oh come on. How are we going to build this road? (*Jimmy goes over to the group, taking the car with him.*)

JIMMY: You building a road?

BILL: Yep.

JIMMY: Hey, that's good. Make it go round here, then we can race round. Let's have some of that. (*Pointing to the clay*)

The two errant players are now fully absorbed into the group. They are making a road. They want to make a road so that they can play more more effectively with their car. This means they must, of necessity, build a good road. It must be of a certain width and have a proper surface. It has to be right.

Suddenly we come to see the operation of a new principle in the class. The work is done because it is necessary, not made necessary by the teacher, not made necessary by some arbiter of curriculum, but necessary because the students think it is. It is their need that creates the criteria for the activity and the good workmanship.

The standards are set by the children, by their necessity. We begin to see the plan of this new lesson coming alive. What we have witnessed is truly motivation.

ARLENE: Miss, I want to make a tree.

TEACHER: Um. You need something for leaves?

ARLENE: Yes. I tried this (*exhibiting crinkled paper*), but it doesn't work too well.

TEACHER: What we want is some of that green plastic stuff they make artificial flowers with.

SANDRA: I could get some. We have lots at home.

ARLENE: Oh good!

TEACHER: You know, we're going to need a lot of different things. How about having a list up on the bulletin board of what we need? Then people can sign up if they can get it for us.

ARLENE: Can I make the list?

TEACHER: Sure you can.

The two girls go off with a large sheet of paper, talking about how to set out the notice. Here the teacher has triggered an activity. Its need is understood by the two children involved. It is not a chore to be performed for the teacher or for the class. It is not a part of any competition for approval. It is a task that fulfills a function that is real to children, not an arbitrary administrative list for the convenience of the teacher. Yet, the way the teacher asked for the list was no different from what might have occurred in a more conventional setting. The difference is not in the asking, but in the understanding that takes place when the asking is done. The asking is done in a different structure. Within this new structure the understanding is about the task, the reasonableness of work. It is a structure that gives all of us, students and teacher, room to learn.

The trestle bridge work area has resolved itself into three groups. Each is working on its own bridges, but all seem to be concerned to do the same things. Each group is making a road leading to the edge of the work surface in both directions from the bridge. The river is centered across the work area. There is competition between the groups as to which will finish first. The activity is a road-building race. Again the teacher observing is uneasy. What is going on is a game. Where is the learning?

JIMMY: We've won! We've won!

DAVID: Our road is better.

JIMMY: No it isn't.

JOEL: Where's the car? Who's got the car?

MICHAEL: Here.

JIMMY: Give it here. Look.

There is general admiration, though the first group goes on making improvements. After a while, when the other two groups have reached a similar stage, the game palls. Then a new suggestion is made:

DAVID: Let's make a road across here.

MICHAEL: Yeah. Let's join this road on, too.

Crossroads joining the three groups are made. This activity occupies several minutes, then two cars are able to meet. The road is not wide enough for them to pass.

DAVID: Let's make the road wider.

MICHAEL: Take that up. We'll start from here.

JIM: I'm going to make a gas station here.

Suddenly the car, the criterion of scale, also dictates land use and building function, and we have an emergent landscape possessed now of both physical and human features.

Two boys work on the gas station:

GLEN: Let's make a space here.

JIM: Why not here? Then we could use both roads. (*Pointing to the corner lot*)

GLEN: O.K. Put the pumps here. This is the highway.

We understand from this conversation germinal economic arguments. As teachers we might well be concerned that children understand the principles of site advantage in economics. Conventionally these advantages would be learned probably by rote from the pages of a textbook no doubt profusely illustrated pictorially and by documentation. Conventionally, too, such information would be appropriate to secondary education, since it would be assumed that the concepts of economics are too abstruse for elementary school children. But in this class we observe children displaying knowledge we certainly have not taught them.

"Put the pumps here. This is the highway." Does this mean what we have assumed it means? It could also be a copy, the orientation of some known gas station, or it could be a recognition that this is the way gas stations are set up. What must be our action now as a teacher? Do we need to verify the understanding of children? Again we find ourselves obsessed with the need to test whether the children really understand, and we are again surprised to discover that the need is really ours. The testing will be for our purposes. Realizing this, we reject our urge and go back to our observations. We are students again.

The gas station is shaping up, but there are construction problems:

GLEN: That's not a proper roof.

JIM: You go make your own.

GLEN: O.K., I will. I'll build a whole new station.

JOEL: Yeah, let's make it here. This'll be good. Just before the bridge. More cars stop here.

DAVE: They got to stop for the toll. We could make some toll booths.

GLEN: Good idea. You do that. We'll do the station. Hey, Miss, we need . . .

There is a sudden deluge of requests for materials. The teacher is now the focus of attention. The teacher is needed. In some strange way a lot of children have turned toward the teacher. First, there was the demand for materials, and then a sort of sympathy swept through the whole group. It is a comfortable feeling, a group reassurance. The group recognizes its leader momentarily and approves. The teacher takes advantage of this momentary leadership:

TEACHER: Arlene is taking care of materials. (*Turns to Arlene*) Isn't that right?

ARLENE: We made a list.

TEACHER: And Sandra, too. It's on the board.

SANDRA: Yeah. People have to sign for what they want.

TEACHER: And other people sign if they can bring it?

SANDRA: Yeah.

TONY: I can bring some wood. My father has a shop in back.

MELVIN: We want some railroad track.

MARK: Yeah, we're going to put a train across our bridge. My brother he's got a model in our basement and . . .

Some people in the class and the teacher drift over to look at what Melvin and Mark are doing:

MELVIN: You see this train's got to come up over here, and these are the yards. It'll be like Chicago.

VALERIE: But I thought that was the George Washington Bridge.

MELVIN: Well, we'll change it. This'll be the city. Only we'll need more space.

MARK: There's another box there.

TEACHER: (*Suddenly aware of the time*) Let's leave that for next time. We can leave the work on the boxes as it is, but the materials must be cleared away now.

A few grumbles are heard from the class. At this point the teacher gives clear directions and the room is restored to its usual order except for the three additional work areas cramping the back aisles.

The class is dismissed, and we are left to reflect upon this second lesson. Melvin's remark stays with us: "This'll be the city."

In our class we are building the city. We are learning to be citizens. We are designers and architects, builders and artisans. Again we discern a direction. We will become inhabitants.

Chapter Five   60

This is an assumption, our assumption. It could become our aim for the next lesson (and maybe for all subsequent lessons). It does not have to be the children's aim. When we look at their work in detail we see many directions.

Let us take first the trestle bridge group with whom we have already spent some time. Work started on three bridges, and the children resolved themselves into three groups, at first competitive. Later, the roads they had made separately were joined, so that, effectively, the work surface became one unit of terrain over which was a road network. Groups then became reformed competitively to build gas stations. The teacher's direction to children was "to build the land." We had in mind that they might come to understand that their concept of a river must have been different from that of other groups, and hence also their understanding of the valley. What they have done is not in opposition to our design; neither is it a direct expression of our aim. What the teacher asked has been fulfilled, yet the aims of children, their self direction, are very different. What has occurred is logical, but the logic does not come from the teacher. It is also clear that at this point, as at the end of our first lesson, we can find the beginning of a new task, a new development. The teacher is not now faced with the problem, "What more can I do?" The children too understand what more to do. In relation to our own learning as teachers, we see that we, like our students, are presented with more learning possibilities. Again let us remember that this lesson, as our first, was designed for precisely this reason, that we might learn.

Let us reiterate our task. We wanted to find a way in which we could develop a method of teaching and a curriculum such that the conventional barriers between teacher and student would not hinder learning. To do this we became students and tried to find a means of communicating with students. A gap was bridged in fact, and it was also the metaphor.

All along we have been uncomfortably aware that while our schemes have worked uncommonly well with respect to methods, the body of information we are as teachers conventionally expected to convey is as elusive as ever. But is it? Maybe we have been looking in the wrong place. We are still assuming that we have the body of information, that it is our job to get it across to children, that it is our job to teach it. When in our efforts to plan this second lesson we tried to think of information which children should have, we seemed to get away from the hard core of subject matter even before we had found it. Now in thinking about this trestle bridge group we see that somehow children have acquired information, or at least used it to build their network of roads and to choose the sites of gas stations. Somehow the information is part of the action, and part of the action, moreover, of the students and not of the teacher. Have we come upon education? Have we rediscovered its meaning? Perhaps. Yet we are rather unwilling to accept this possibility. After all, the children must somehow have acquired the information they applied. This is precisely the assumption that teachers work with when they ask questions of children. The question and answer sessions, the introductory motivational procedures of the conventional lesson, are designed to bring out what is intuitively known, to make rational the half-formed notion, to create a structural lattice of reason from the bits and pieces of experience. Theoretically we recognize the grand idea, but in practice how commonly destructive the procedure is. Children, in this second lesson, are performing what previously we would have required them to think, and to state in words. Conventionally they are required to be rational and literate, and in our new scheme we are using a vulgar form and manual skills. Far from introducing into our classes a new and improved technique, it seems we have retrogressed and abandoned reason and the intellect. So may we argue, with some dismay.

Let us look at our argument again. We were trying to find the source of information. It seems to emanate from the children. In the conventional structure the idea is to find out what children know, to make them realize what they know, and then to add to that knowledge a further distinct body of information to be given by the teacher. Now in this, the second, lesson we have discovered the knowledge that children have, but we still have not yet found a way to transmit additional knowledge. Moreover, it looks as though the kind of knowledge the children have is not held in common by the class, but by a few individuals, and second, it may be even that this knowledge is not at a conscious, intelligible level.

Looked at in this way our actions as teachers are clearly suspect. We are not doing our job. And yet we started out along this path of exploration because in the old scheme of things, though in one sense we were doing the job, we were not accomplishing its purposes.

Let us look at what we have accomplished in our new way. Since we started out, at the beginning of that first lesson, to build bridges, we have become aware of material changes in the class. In two lessons we have acquired more "furniture," more work space, and actual working models. There have been functional changes, too. Children are taking responsibility for planning and implementation, not because it is demanded of them but because it is seen as a "natural function" of the work task. The emotional climate of the class is different; the focus of attention is the task, not the teacher, nor the students, and the task is getting done. The level of performance has gone up, and the standard of its achievement is measured by the achievers. There is a sense, too, of progression, of movement, of possibilities. There is a new dynamic in the class, in students and teacher alike.

On the one hand our achievements in the space of two lessons are massive, and yet we still feel the need to justify and to argue about our role in all this in conventional terms. Maybe this is what is holding up our learning. We are still involved with the conventional criteria. We are still wanting to teach, to convey information. Let us then commit ourselves again firmly to the role of student. Let us remember that our object is to learn. Let us look at what has happened and see what we can understand.

So far we have examined only the trestle bridge group. Let us look now at the George Washington Bridge group. It is this group that had become the focus of attention at the end of the lesson. Melvin was wanting railroad track for "Chicago," and in describing the work of the group he said, "This'll be the city."

When we look at the work surface of this group it is clear that the bridges have ceased to be the focus of attention. The river now has curves and a tributary. It has banks backed by a flat area of cardboard on which is drawn out roughly the site of a railroad, and sidings. The best bridge still stands, and some attempt has been made to fix it in place. The two other bridges are movable and belong to no fixed site. In one corner it looks as though there has been some independent operation. A skeleton map has been drawn of city blocks, and one block is filled with what looks like an attempted high rise. A piece of foolscap has been folded and glued upright. Windows have been penciled roughly on the outside. This group too has built the land.

The third group work surface has no bridges left. The river winds and there are high banks with a landing stage at one place where a very superior ferryboat is tied up. Paper people are standing on the banks, and behind them are primitive paper trees. This must have been what Arlene and Sandra were wanting to improve.

It begins to appear as though our early assumption that each group would produce a different terrain is going to turn out in fact. But we are still uneasy. What has been made is really very messy. There is no coherent over-all plan. It may be helpful to know that we have a direction, and to see that each group of children also has a direction, but we should certainly be more comfortable if we really knew what we were doing. It's true that we are trying to find out, but just how long can we go on like this? How long ought we to go on like this? This second lesson in some ways has been more taxing than the first. Although the children know their task, we do not yet understand ours. This threatens our comfort and security. Our role is to learn, to be a student, but what do we do? The one point in the lesson which for the teacher, for us, was the most comfortable moment was when suddenly our attention was demanded and children expressed their wants in short-order material terms. One thing we can do is supply those needs. Can we go one step further and anticipate them? In the third lesson what will be their needs, that is, their material needs? Obviously, building materials. Suddenly it seems as though our project is arts and crafts and that what we are doing is simply building bigger and better models. Models of what? Not of bridges, not anymore. Buildings, roads, trees, people, landscapes, human habitats. Suddenly we see again what the work of the class may signify. What is being built is a metaphor for human society. We started with the notion of creating a metaphor for communication, a gap to be bridged, and now suddenly we see that the children have gone far beyond our own limited version and are building a multifaceted model of the totality of human experience. Do they know this? Do they need to know it?

Again we suddenly feel the urge to communicate our understandings. We want to formulate information for others. And again we are struck by the fact that we want to tell children about themselves, about what they have done. This was the object of our second lesson. At a conscious level, at least, we did not succeed, and yet we see that the outcome of the lesson could in no way be called a failure because this aim failed. Are we then to set off in the third lesson to try to do a similar thing? Maybe we have to give up judging what we think it would be good for students to know. This would mean abandoning entirely the idea of curriculum. Theoretically we thought we had already abandoned the curriculum for our first two lessons, but the pattern of our thinking is still operating in terms of a curriculum. No blame attaches to this. It is simply a fact we now can recognize.

We are aware that our thinking in many ways is altering, but we must not be surprised to find that our learning is being held back by habits we have never been fully aware of until now.

We are excited by finding the metaphor made by children. This is our discovery. It is our learning. It does not have to be, nor need to be, the learning of the children. Their purposes are different from ours. We all need to learn, but we do not need to learn the same things. This applies not simply to the children and ourselves but to children individually. In theory the conventional teacher knows this very well. We have the advantage of being able to operate practically. We still have to ask ourselves, "How?" and it seems suspiciously as though we are beginning to ask our old question again, "What more can I do?" We should not be too surprised by this. We know that in learning there are periods of rapid progress and plateaus of protracted sameness. Sometimes there is retrogression. We are learning now. It is natural for us suddenly to understand, and then to feel dull and stupid about what to do next. Our advantage is that we now know how to begin, that is, to start from where we are and with what we know. So, we must provide a variety of materials for building. We need wood, paper, cloth, oak tag, paints, glue, boxes. We need junk.

Young children play happily with a stick and an old can. They will play for hours with a discarded radio. They will play for days on a sandy beach with or without pail and shovel. What we need in the classroom is the equivalence of these materials. Again we may feel some hesitancy. It is true that children play with these things, but do we want children to play? Are we really asking them to play at making models? Let us suppose that this is what we are doing, that this is what we have done. We can look at the material results and see a mess, the kind of mess that happens in play, and we could be convinced of our error, or we could look, as we have done, at the kinds of thinking, understood from conversation, that have gone into the creation of the mess. The thinking has not been trivial. It has been serious, geared for the most part to the solving of problems, the expression of needs, the formulation of ideas, the communication of values and of value judgments. If this is all a part of play, let us continue our play.

So, we need junk. It may seem strange to us that children naturally like junk. Perhaps it is because they can emulate the adult world with the castoffs from it. From an archaeological point of view we might understand it in another way, the new generation taking the waste of its predecessors to build the foundations for a new city. This is something we might be concerned to teach in these antipollution days, the recycling of waste materials. But all this is again our understanding as a teacher, and it will not necessarily become the understanding of our students. Nonetheless, if we use junk, and if we do not waste new materials, children will acquire by working alongside of us habits of conservation and a knowledge of how to use and reuse. In any case they will learn how to use what they have because they have nothing else.

We may at this point begin to see ourselves in a new way, as something children "have." We are used to the question asked by students at the beginning of a new term or semester: "Who is your teacher this year?" "What teacher do you have?" Somehow as teachers we have, most of us, never really understood that we are there for students to have. What would we have them have? What do we have to give? Our answer in conventional terms is obvious: information. And clearly, the more information we have, the better we are equipped as a teacher. But very early in our discussions we found that the problem is in the giving of this information. What we have may very well be the antithesis of what the student wants to have. Can we now reform our answer?

The provision of materials must take place before the lesson. It belongs, therefore, to the planning stage. What we are trying to do now is to find out whether we can use ourselves as something children can have in the lesson. Clearly, they can call upon us as a resource, and in this sense we are like a book, a repository of information, but this is not the active having linked with the active doing that children will incorporate into their learning.

We found the second lesson to be a more difficult experience than the first, mainly because our involvement was much less. Hence we have sought to discover what it is we might do. So far our doing has been planning, the planning of material provisions. Now it looks as if what we do in the lesson has somehow to be linked with the children's capacity to have us as an active participant. In that first lesson we built. Can we in the next lesson build again? In order for children to learn from us, to have information from us, must we practice some skill about which we are informed or through which we can inform them? In addition, for example, to asking of students a specific task, can we ourselves perform a specific task which exhibits the information we should like children to have? In our first lesson we did do exactly what we wanted children to do, namely, bridge the gap. In our next lesson we should like to develop the city. By so doing we hope that we shall be developing citizens.

There are three work areas in the room, the road network group (formerly the trestle bridge group), the city group (formerly the George Washington Bridge group), and the rural scene group. If we actively join forces with the city group, we shall be doing a disservice to the other groups, so clearly, we need to find a way of assisting the whole by performing a function not yet apparent in the present activities.

Though each group can effectively work at its project and develop its latent possibilities, it would be advantageous to the class as a whole if each group could, if it felt the need, in some way relate to the others. What we need, then, is some way of making the now-separate work tasks into a coherent whole. We need, as it were, to extend the boundaries of our planning to encompass all the activities. We know that it will be our plan, that it may never become the plan of the children, but while they have their frame of reference, the particularity of their own group, we shall have ours, a boundary condition within which we can work. We shall at last know more firmly what it is we are doing. At last, then, we have found a way to formulate our problem, and since we now know what our problem is, we are approaching its solution.

The function of the teacher in our new operation is becoming clearer. First, materials are needed. This is a planning function.

Second, during the lesson the teacher must actively perform some work which will give coherence to the diverse operations of the student groups. This involves us in looking for relations. Presently, we have before us the road network group, the city group with its railroad, and the rural scene group. To build a coherent and supportive structure into which these three groups can fit involves the use, for example, of area on a larger scale than used by one group alone. Thus we could make an analogy such that:

CITY GROUP	EQUATED WITH	CITY
ROAD NETWORK GROUP	EQUATED WITH	SUBURBS
RURAL SCENE GROUP	EQUATED WITH	COUNTRY

There is an equivalence to type areas of human occupancy. The groups could be linked together in the classroom by creating a model transection of an actual piece of land. Thus on the classroom wall the teacher might put up a display, during the heat of the lesson, of maps and pictures illustrative of city, suburbs, and country and relocate the three work areas to conform with this structure. In this way the gaps between the work areas, between the models, would become apparent, and these would become the new bridging points. The bridges thus become actual informational areas, and we begin to see whence information derives. When a gap is seen then information is needed to fill it. The information comes from whatever lies on either side of the gap. Thus the construction of the bridge is both the method and the curriculum. This is precisely what we have been looking for, precisely why we built those first bridges. When we were looking for information previously we could not find it because it was being used. The traveler who is traveling no longer needs the schedule giving him the information about when he must travel. We have been the travelers traveling. We have been aware of motion. We have been sensitive to progression. In our conventional class these things did not happen, though we had the schedule. It was read. It was information, but no informing took place. There was no gap to be filled, no space for the information to flow into, to fill. There was no gap because students and teacher were unaware of it. The students were on one side, unable to see the other, and the teacher was on the other side, unable to be with the students. The preoccupation was with sides, to be against. There was only an opposition to be overcome, not something to be bridged, something to be informed about, something to mediate communication.

Our discoveries have become possible only because we the teachers have become students and behave as students. That is, we are prepared to learn. Our prime task, if we are truly teachers, is simply to learn, not in private but in public, not in the seclusion of our studies and in extension classes and after-school programs and all the rest but in our own classrooms with our classes, with our students. And it is our learning that is important, our learning about ourselves and for ourselves, not our learning about the students or for the students. They and they alone must do their own learning. They will learn about us, as students always learn about their teachers, and because of this they will learn that we learn, and even what we learn. They will learn along with us.

If we think again for a moment of Melvin's remark, "This'll be the city," and come to understand the metaphor of the work in the class, that a city is being built, that the students are the citizens, we may come to realize how it is that we the teachers have had such a hard time trying to define our role and function in the group. Part of our difficulty must be that there is not in the city a leader analogous in role and function to the teacher of this class. This is what we are trying to find—a new form of leadership. No wonder we are having a hard time! The amount of learning we have to do is truly phenomenal, but just think what we have already learned— the need and reason for our search for a new role. When genuine learning takes place the behavior of the learner changes. We are learning. Our behavior is changing. The children are learning. Their behavior is changing. Excitement, even fear, we may feel. All we can do is to go on learning. Let us ride the impetus of change.

Looking back, we wonder how this thought did not strike us before. The problems of leadership in the city are constantly with us, as have been the concerns of authority in the classroom. Yet it is not so strange that we failed earlier to make the connection, since we are still unused to our role of student in the class. It is only from the standpoint of a student that we can look and see the teacher of the class as ruler. When you are the ruler you know your task and don't question it; you are concerned only with how to do it. When we become students, then we are as other citizens, looking for leadership.

It now appears to us that if we persist in our role of student, the other students will be forced to learn something about leadership, which will be very different from learning about tyranny and the role of the one, however good. Our leadership will consist in being the prime learner. It is not easy to know whether this equates with democracy. Perhaps it is a new form of government which teachers will teach.

We have submitted to the learning process and we are learning. Our learning is full of surprises. We could not have conceived in advance a curriculum for it, and yet it seems that what we are learning is of the utmost importance to us especially as teachers. Could it be also the same for children, that what they are learning, that is, what each one of them individually is learning, has no place in a contrived curriculum? We seem now to be back to our familiar problem area, of content and information. But we are wiser now and know how to deal with it, temporarily at least. So let us become again students and think out how we can forward our aims in the coming lesson.

We wanted to demonstrate an equivalence between the models and three modes of human occupancy—rural, suburban, and urban. The transection gives us an over-all structure, yet it may also be thought too neat, too packaged, too simplified, too complex, or too sophisticated for children. Whether it is so depends upon our level of understanding of the relations involved and upon our degree of training in specific fields. But as we have seen in each of our earlier lessons, our understanding and levels of comprehension do not limit those of students, if we are a student, nor do we force students to accept ideas which, though they came out of college the year before last, may already be, indeed almost certainly are, for the most part, obsolete. What we have done is to make a structure in which we can operate, in which we can practice the skills we have, and through which children may come to comprehend more than we understand, and comprehend also in ways different from the teacher's. From both our previous lessons more has come than we were able to anticipate. Much has come as a result of the diversity of doing and thinking. The collected intelligence far outweighs the single understanding of the teacher. That is why the teacher has to be the prime learner. In order for that great reservoir of intelligence to be mobilized, made to move productively, it is necessary for the teacher to be seen learning, to be seen doing.

In the next lesson the teacher must be seen creating the transection, arranging maps and pictures and diagrams and the like, ordering visually the idea, and leaving gaps. The children will not necessarily understand the idea, nor do we necessarily want them to. It is the teacher's idea, subject to confusions, inaccuracies, obsolescence. But where there is the beginning of order children will find their own beginning and create the new order.

Still, for some teachers there are doubts. Do such procedures really produce learning situations? Do children really learn? Let us look at lesson three.

The teacher has set out the three work areas at the back of the room. The bulletin boards are bare. There are materials set out in neat piles to which children may help themselves. The lesson begins with a brief word from the teacher, who asks simply that students continue with their projects. The teacher then goes to the back of the room and pins up a large picture of downtown Chicago and some travel brochures with more city pictures. Steve approaches the teacher, stands for a moment, looks at the pictures, and looks up at the teacher, who smiles. He hesitates, then goes on rather stolidly looking at the pictures again. The teacher goes on with her work. This moment is crucial. It would be so easy for the teacher to behave in the conventional way, to ask a question about the pictures, to incorporate the student into her activity. It would be so easy to justify such an action in conventional terms. It would be so easy to destroy the initiative of the student. Wisely, the teacher stays out of the student's way and leaves the decisions to the student. She goes on with her own activity, putting up pictures.

In a little while Steve is joined by another student. Almost immediately there is conversation:

KEVIN: That's nice.

STEVE: Yeah.

KEVIN: I'd like to live there.

STEVE: In Chicago?

KEVIN: No, in there.

An Explosion of Learning   71

TEACHER: A high rise.

KEVIN: Yep. You been in one?

TEACHER: I live in one.

KEVIN: You're kidding.

TEACHER: No, really, . . . and we can see the airport way in the distance.

KEVIN: And airplanes. Can you see them land? I want to fly . . .

Kevin launches into a frenzied catalog of the kinds of planes he wants to fly, where he wants to fly, how fast, and at what altitude. To the teacher the classroom seems terribly confining and a hopelessly inadequate place for helping Kevin to realize even the smallest part of his desires. It is imperative to do something right now. The teacher has no materials. She sits down at an empty desk with Kevin and Steve, with pencil and paper, and thinks aloud.

TEACHER: I really don't know too much about airplanes, but I've been to a lot of airports. Usually there is an entrance here like this (*draws a plan*), and down here the various airlines have their ticket counters. What you do is . . .

KEVIN: Gee.

STEVE: And if the wind is blowing this way they use this runway?

TEACHER: Yes.

STEVE: What happens if a plane crashes and they can't?

TEACHER: They've got problems!

STEVE: Yeah, but what do they do, really?

TEACHER: Fly around in circles.

STEVE: No. Tell me.

TEACHER: Really, that's what they do.

The thing to do now is to make the problem, to set a theoretical number of planes, with theoretical amounts of reserve fuel, flight capabilities, and so on, and then to see what can be done. The children begin to see what questions to ask, what information they want (in this case, what they need to invent). They understand what it is they want to know, and they understand how to use information before they have it. This is very different from the conventional order of learning, which insists first on the acquisition of information and later (often much later, sometimes after the the student has left school) on the ability and skill to use it. Hence teachers can say, "I cannot teach area because they can't multiply."

It is true that in the classroom the actual situation created and the methods of its solution will be a long way from the live experience of an airport, just as building bridges in the class has been a long way short of the bridge builders' reality. But bridge building was not our curriculum, nor is the logistics of flight planning. These activities are metaphors. So for the moment we need not be overly concerned with technical limitations.

While the teacher has been working with the two boys the other groups have been working along on their own. Arlene and Sandra have been planting "trees," with very interesting results:

SANDRA: This is too big.

ARLENE: What d'you mean?

SANDRA: It's too big.

GARY: It makes the boat all wrong.

ARLENE: Take the boat away, then.

GARY: Stupid. (*Neal picks up the boat.*)

GARY: Where you going?

NEAL: (*Puts the boat back*) It's the river.

ARLENE: What's he talking about? (*Neal starts to take away part of the bank opposite the trees.*)

Some time later this group is observed by the teacher to have remodeled their work surface and added to it another unit area (box) so that the relative sizes of trees, boat, and river width are more appropriate. Two boys have spent some time arguing about the name of the boat and are now seated separately from the group drawing pictures of river boats complete with paddle wheels. Arlene and Sandra have had such success with their tree planting that they start working with the suburbs group on making a park. This group too has split up. The gas station builders are now busy creating a shopping plaza, while the road racers have set up independently and are making a special track.

When the teacher leaves the boys creating their airport problem she is immediately drawn into the race track group. It appears they want a map of Le Mans, which one of them remembers having seen in a book in the library. The teacher leaves them working on a large chart listing the names of contestants, their cars, laps, standings in the race, and so on.

Almost immediately the teacher becomes involved in the city group. It appears that Chicago has been scrapped! Instead, our city is being built. There is tremendous difficulty simply because the children are unable to agree where things go:

MELVIN: The station goes here.

MARK: No it doesn't. That's where the river is.

VALERIE: The river goes by the station.

MARK: No, not there, the other side.

VALERIE: It does not.

Fortunately, the teacher has an old street map, somewhat battered and very hard to read, but at least the river is clear. There is more wrangling and then agreement about where the station is. Melvin and Mark reorient their track and start building it again. Others in the group feel they are not wanted and cluster around the teacher, all of them momentarily lost. Mary looks up at the partially completed bulletin board, and the teacher asks if she would like to sort through the pile of pictures and decide on an arrangement. She goes off and is joined by Tana. The teacher takes pencil and paper, sits down, and draws a city block:

TEACHER: This is the school. Here's the front entrance.

MYRA: I live right across, there.

In a very short time the really important part of our city is drawn out. It soon becomes obvious that nothing short of a real scale model will satisfy:

MYRA: It's got to be right.

The children argue about the parking lot and the teacher leaves them measuring all the model cars they can find to decide what scale they will use.

Two girls are standing arm in arm watching Melvin and Mark. June glances up as the teacher passes:

JUNE: They look just like real workers, Miss.

TEACHER: Um, yes. You look like real lookers on. (*They all laugh.*)

JUNE: Someone ought to come along and interview us. (*Pause. The teacher, on a sudden thought, picks up a ruler and and hands it to June.*)

TEACHER: Here's the microphone. (*June takes it. Giggles*)

JUNE: I couldn't.

TEACHER: Maybe you'd rather be a newspaper reporter.

SUSAN: Yeah. O.K., we'll be reporters. We'll write a real good story. (*More laughter*)

A lesson that was brought to being with agonies of effort ends with laughter. The children have gone. The teacher laughs to herself. It's "a real good story." The planning of the lesson now seems academic. Even retrospectively we shall have a problem trying to summarize what happened. There is math in a dozen different forms, reading, writing, discussion, history, geography, engineering, town planning, social studies, landscape "gardening," graphic arts, and so on. There has been a veritable explosion of learning in the class.

CHAPTER SIX

Learning Habitats

"It's a real good story," and to judge from the teacher's reaction, it has a happy ending. Genuine laughter and lightheartedness are rare commodities in the classroom. Yet education need not be such a serious business. There is no reason why children and teachers can't have a thoroughly good time in their classes together. In our three lessons we have witnessed a very rapid growth in the social intercourse of the class, and we have seen, finally, that a teacher and a child can communicate with a real sense of equality. Alongside a new-found sense of ease, we have seen children following a huge range of interests that spread out and encompass far more than the prescribed curriculum areas. The conventional basic skills are used to describe, record, and enumerate their experiences, and we see all aspects in operation at the same time. This totality is apparent to even casual observation. It could almost be photographed. Those who have come with us through this experience will recognize the totality at another level. It is in the work task of the class, in each group separately, and in the class as a whole. The work the class does is a metaphor also of a totality, of the city, of human habitats. The work task mediates between the real life of the city and the real life of the class. A conventional curriculum which is essentially a breakdown of subject areas, which are themselves a breakdown, does not and cannot be a mediator between what is known in the city and what must become known by the youth of the city. Where there is no mediation there is confrontation. Thus we distinguish the essential difference between the kinds of lessons which we described in the conventional system and the three lessons in which the teacher's prime aim was to learn.

Before we develop further the three-lesson campaign and examine how within the regular school setting—the conventional system —the teacher and the children can continue their learning, we shall elaborate our present stage of achievement. Our aim is, as always, to try to understand what we are doing. In the conventional lesson the teacher assumes an understanding, assumes she is teaching spellings or the use of commas, or whatever, when in fact the learning going on concerns how to deal with authority in various ways, not least to play up to the assumptions of the teacher. We are not under the assumption of working at building bridges or cities or whatever it may be. Our work is not curriculum based. We did not ask children to learn about airports or trains or scheduling or scale drawing or map making or whatever, not to write, nor to practice math skills, yet all of these things are happening. It seems there has been a release of learning energy. For the outpouring of creativity in the class to continue, for the explosive learning energy to find fulfillment, we had better try to see what it is we are doing.

We have noted already the development of certain characteristics, the diversity of tasks performed, the changing roles within groups and between groups. We notice things our professional training tells us to notice, but there is something else that the casual observer will be quick to see, and that is simply the general conduct of the children. They are not behaving as they would in a regular class. They are arguing, joking, teasing, talking earnestly with one another, being concerned with one another. They are living.

It is this sense of living that gives us the clue to what is happening. Life, in whatever form, begins and grows and multiplies and is related to the forms around it. It is not an isolated entity—or if it is, it dies. To live and to learn is the natural order. What teachers have tried to do is to cultivate the learning. They have done this by subduing certain living relations. Educators have been planting children in rows and telling them to grow in certain ways. This has produced on the one hand people dedicated to the status quo and on the other a lot of rebels.

The problem here is that the confrontation learned in school is carried over and becomes a way of life, and ultimately a way of destruction. The one thing which resolves the confrontation is the gap where learning can take place by being bridged, the gap which we have bridged, where information now flows, and where new relations can be established. Whenever there is learning there is movement and change, and there are possibilities. There is mediation. Educators then need concern themselves with one thing, and one thing only—that students should know what it means to learn.

This statement looks simple almost to the point of absurdity. All educators will say that this is precisely what they do, that their students do know how to learn, that the whole trend of modern education has been toward encouraging the student to find out for himself. Certainly this is the case. Students search diligently for information in the library, in reference books and scholarly journals. They have the information on the best authority, but they do not have it on their own authority. They do not know what it means to learn themselves.

It is obviously useful, essential even, to know how to get information. Ours is the era of the information explosion. This needs to be matched with a learning explosion, which, as we have seen, is not at all the same thing.

It is not the same thing because it involves an individual in a live situation. The learning and the living have to go together. Books can be stacked in a library and information can be stacked in a bank. Learning is not static, nor can it be stacked. Thus if students are to have knowledge of learning, there must be inherent in the learning situation a complexity of relations analogous to those of an ecological system. There must be a totality of interdependence. The information is in the system, in the habitat, and so are the students, so is the teacher. In the three lessons we witnessed the growth of a habitat: first the bridge, then the valley, then a city, its environs and hinterland. These were creations initiated by the teacher and presented by her, but developed only by being inhabited by students. It is the exploration of the habitat that signifies learning.

At this point it might appear that we have developed a new scheme for lesson planning. Instead of the teacher being asked to go through a procedure of "motivation" and "initial activity" and all the rest, the teacher is, instead, being asked to create a "habitat"; in other words, it seems that the old formula is being cloaked in new words. But this is by no means the case. The whole point about habitats is that they are created by the people—students and teachers —who learn in them.

Young children are very good at creating habitats. Given a typewriter, a six-year-old will play office for hours. At first he makes little attempt to type real words, but once a certain degree of manual dexterity has been achieved real words, starting often with the child's own name, become very important to the child. Copying is carried on in fact and in metaphor. An old stethoscope provokes an elaborate hospital game. Bits of wood and an iron bar in the backyard become a building site, a city block, gang territory. Whenever children play "let's pretend," they create a totality, a whole office with a work complex, a whole hospital with patients and doctors. They don't stay with one job, with one function, with one anything. They play many parts, they explore every corner of the habitat. They don't learn one thing simply, but many things, all at once, interrelatedly. They learn how to be and how to do.

Again we understand how this kind of learning contrasts with the kind of learning possible in the conventional class and the set lesson. Take first the being. Even if students have the very best teacher and are given the very best lesson, they are still students, and the teacher is still teacher. The roles are fixed. When a point of difference is reached there is either submission or conflict. No other choice is available. To help overcome the problems of understanding other points of view role-playing, as a technique, has been developed in some schools, often with markedly beneficial results. Recalcitrant students are asked to be the teacher, and the teacher plays the role of student. But still there are only two roles. The best conventionally is not good enough for a learning explosion. In a habitat roles change constantly and in their variety are limited only by the limitations of the learners. Learning cannot be limited by the teacher if the teacher is also learner-in-chief.

The learning to be, then, is limited in the set lesson. What about the learning to do? It would be easy to take as an example of limitation the inability of a set lesson to provide for an opportunity for doing construction work. To be fair, then, let us take an example in which the conventional classroom takes some pride, namely, the teaching of listening skills (and we are not poking fun at the teacher who has constantly to say, "Be quiet"; "Listen").

The following observations were made in a second grade class in an inner-city school. The teacher is one of the best, well liked by her students, by their parents, and by the rest of the faculty. She has had many years of experience and is a thoroughly competent teacher, not ambitious for advancement in the school organization but very concerned for the well-being of students in her care. For the first activity in the afternoon she has planned a lesson in the science series on sound. The film projector is set up and alongside it the tape recorder with appropriate dialogue. The children enter quietly and sit in their assigned places ready to begin. This is obviously a well-organized, well-conducted class. The teacher, in a gentle, friendly voice explains, "This afternoon we are going to watch a filmstrip about sounds. The sounds will be explained by a tape. Listen carefully and do what you are asked." The first picture comes on the screen. It is a farm animal. Sounds come from the tape, and a voice asks, "What animal makes this sound?" The class in unison replies, "A cow." There is a pause and the tape goes on, "A cow. Well done." (The observer reflects on the irrelevance of cows to inner-city children; he notes the inevitable question and the praise for docility. But maybe it will get better.) This pattern is repeated some twenty times, using as examples animals, street sounds, warning noises, weather sounds, and so on. Sometimes there are humorous juxtapositions, and the class laughs. The lesson lasts about twenty-five minutes. The teacher terminates it by asking more questions, about loud sounds and soft sounds, until she is certain that the children have all grasped the concept of sound. Then she says, "All right, now we'll change the subject. It's time for phonics.

This is one of many observed examples. It is quoted because it occurred in the class of a respected teacher and a highly intelligent woman. For her, sound is science and phonics is language arts. No link is thought of. No link is thinkable. Thus learning to do what absolutely has to be done in all conventional classes, that is, listen, is also strictly limited. Roles are set. Subjects are set. It is useless to argue flexibility because the unthinkable can't be flexed.

Let us return to our examination of habitats. In each of the lessons the teacher miscalculated the diversity, the complexity of the habitat the learners together would build. Complexity seems to be necessary for learning, and the complexity has somehow to be evolved by the learners, not necessarily out of simplicity but by social interaction, by living together. In a sense the learning is a recognition of what already is.

Perhaps we can begin to understand something about what happened in the third lesson. The teacher began with her task, which she never got around to completing. Each time she was interrupted she was taken into a group to help with problem-solving. She was not asked to solve problems, nor was it always clear who had the problem. Just there was a problem. The teacher sat down with pencil and paper and thought, and talked, and in the thinking and talking there grew a habitat. The teacher did what children do. The teacher used her own experience, and her own inexperience. She used herself. She felt she had to do something. This you will remember had been the problem after lesson two, namely, what to do in the lesson. The teacher doodled, with words, with ideas, with associations.

At the end of the lesson there was so much diversity, so many different kinds of work tasks, that for the children, it may be argued, there could be no pretense of an over-all coherence, a totality, a habitat. Here once again we are faced with the duality of teaching and learning signified by the gap. But it is there only when the teacher is unable to be a student. The habitat can be thought of as the transection through rural, suburban, and urban modes. This may be academic. This habitat is, after all, the one the teacher uses to orient her own learning aims, which, as we have seen, may be very different—and rightly so—from those of children. Within this habitat are smaller units to be explored. Other designs may occur which lie way outside the teacher's range, as they did in lessons one and two, and as we have seen, the teacher learns from these to extend the boundaries and use them as conditions for her own learning. A habitat, then, is not fixed and immutable. It changes and grows as do the people—the learners—who live in it. Things, places, people, functions, and roles are integrated.

The deliberate attempt by educators to create a totality within the classroom has come to be called the integrated day program. It is also variously and loosely equated with the open classroom, the

British infant school, and the Leicestershire plan. Programs of this kind have been developed in Great Britain, initially with children in the five-to-seven-year range, called infants, and later throughout primary education. The new open approach began largely as an invention of necessity, in a period of national crises. Acute shortages of basic materials such as paper and books, and of teachers, made it necessary for children to help one another, for teachers to make their own teaching aids, and for children to help teachers to do this. Children responded well in this situation, and in spite of shortages it appeared that the over-all quality of primary education improved. Most children learned to read and to read well, though if asked, few teachers were able to say how this had happened. As a result of changes in classroom practice, teacher-training programs positively endorsed curriculum overlap. This gave rise to a diversity among colleges of education, responsible for the training of primary school teachers, as well as among instructors at individual colleges. These factors, in turn, produced large numbers of newly qualified teachers with diverse experiences willing to create in their own classes new kinds of learning situations for children.

The diversity was principally curricular. For example, instead of using conventional subject matters a theme would be chosen— "whales," let us say. During the course of a week, or maybe more, children would be expected to:

1. Write about whales—where they lived, moved, and had their being.
2. Calculate their size, weight, displacement, quantity of food consumed per period of time, speed of movement, distance traveled, and so forth.
3. Listen to famous stories about whales.
4. Reenact scenes from *Moby Dick*.
5. Dance and mime, using techniques of modern dance.
6. Read and write poems.
7. Draw and paint related themes.
8. Listen to the "Antarctic Symphony."

It would not matter whether these children were five or six or nine or ten. Their achievements would be simply what they could do. For a period of time all their school activities would be related to the theme. Some teachers found it possible to have drawing and painting and listening and writing and calculating all going on at the same time. Others used the theme much as a regular curiculum to have formal periods of writing or of listening. All of this tended to induce a hearty dislike of whales, which theme was then replaced by another, and so on. The current of understanding, however, aided these teachers, so that even the most formal among them generally succumbed to a period of "free activity" at the beginning of the morning and afternoon sessions. At these times children finished off whatever projects they wished, so that gradually arts and crafts activities became associated with writing and calculating, and these latter became also subjects able to be discussed informally. The free-activity periods became extended, because most teachers recognized that it was at this time that the most learning took place. Also, what had once seemed to them to be the most difficult kind of situation to control now had become the easiest and happiest part of the school day, for them and for the children.

Subsequently, the strict thematic adherence was dropped, mainly as a result again of the free-activity periods. The activities engaged in by children became genuinely free in the sense that they quite happily developed their own particular interests. Children, for example, would bring objects to school, talk about things they did at home, and so come to use these aspects of their experience as a basis for further investigation. Generally speaking, this had nothing to do with whales. The investigations of the children brought into the classroom a great variety of books, often too difficult for immediate comprehension, but which somehow they managed to use. Once there, books and other things that children brought in or made tended to stay around and thus provided materials for others to study. In this way parts of the room tended to be set aside for special tasks. All the measuring things were put in one place. Books were kept somewhere else, and, of course, animals and paints and clay were separate too. Most students in training for teaching now go through required courses in how to set up a room and equip it in this fashion.

What is now known as the integrated day is, then, very largely a matter of happy accident. Educators are presently trying to turn that accident into a program, trying to formulate it and systematize it because it works. When the accident has been sufficiently elaborated with conventions, it will have become educationally useless.

The integration is not really a totality in the way in which we conceive a habitat. There is a relation established between basic skills and some kind of informational material, "whales" or "food" or "ports" or whatever, but the human—the social—relations, the market place learning, this dimension is almost wholly absent from the design, though not always in its implementation, in both the actual school classroom and the educational program of prospective teachers. The accident lives because of its diversity and hence its possibilities for continuous change. When these become prescribed, then its dynamic will cease.

The integrated day program works for great numbers of students and teachers, but for American teachers there are major drawbacks. It developed in a foreign country in which school conditions and educational perceptions are very different. It cannot therefore be copied, and translations are notoriously imperfect. But more important, though its success lies in its diversity and in its ability to integrate diversity, it is a program limited by its conception of a social order. It is a radical improvement, not a radical change. The school place and the school society are basic to its operation.

The developments that we have witnessed from the three lessons, while they begin to look very much like the kinds of things that happen in the operation of the integrated day program, have a very different base. We are still in the class, in the school, and working within the conventional hierarchical social system because we must start where we are, and that is the place and the position where we are. But the base of our thinking and hence of our operations is independent of these conditions, excepting only in their physical presence. Our base was not dependent upon information, curricular or thematic, subject oriented or integrated. It was not dependent upon our being a teacher, but simply upon our own desire to learn. Our problem was to discover what we wanted to learn and how to learn it, and as we began to learn these two problems ceased to be. Both curriculum and method became unimportant. Retrospectively we could look back and give form to both. They could be perceived historically, after the event. In this way they became information, that is, after the informing took place.

The term "open classroom" is really descriptive of what a classroom comes to look like in the integrated day program. It looks like the kind of thing that has developed in the three lessons. It is full of a lot of people doing a lot of different things at one and the same time. We now have an open classroom in this sense, and we have it because we have been able to open our minds to learning. We have come in our understanding to see how, in what we have called a habitat, learning takes place, rapidly advancing in many directions at once. We have seeen that this appears in some ways like the integrated day program of British primary schools, but that the principles upon which the three lessons have been based are very different. If this is indeed the case, we should expect that what we are presently doing will continue to develop and come to look very different from the integrated day program. Our policy then is to go ahead with our own program of learning, continuing the search for a new dynamic. What we wish for our students we must practice ourselves. We must be our own authority for our own learning.

We shall proceed with our three-lesson campaign.

CHAPTER SEVEN

School Without Lessons

We left our teacher at the end of the third lesson in a somewhat unusual state. She was laughing. A serious-minded administrator, a supervisor, a vice-principal, would find it hard to see any humor in the situation. He would be confronted by a room full of activity and purpose and yet not be able to get any satisfactory answers about purposes. The lesson plan would not help him. It would not yet have been written. The specific task of the teacher in the lesson was never accomplished. To him it would look as though no lesson was taking place at all. And, indeed, while we have been very concerned to describe the course of three lessons, there is a sense in which the notion of lesson has disappeared. We have instead established a habitat within which to work. And we understand this to be a very real framework against whose boundaries we, the students, can test ourselves, but which also protects us from spatial chaos and anarchy and which, furthermore, grows with us as we grow because we are a part of it. This understanding has come about through our learning in the classroom, and we are not going to sound very convincing to the school official. Hopefully, and we are going to assume this is the case, he will not yet have arrived on the scene, but clearly if we are going to persist with our learning, we are also going to have to find ways of protecting ourselves. The confrontation which formerly existed between the children and ourselves has shifted. It is now we who confront the school authority. There is a new gap to be bridged, and it is we who are going once again to have to learn how to do it. And yet, if we think about it further, it is really not for us to take responsibility for the learning of the administrators, any more than it was the responsibility of the children to take care of our learning. Again we see very clearly that in a true learning community it is the task of those whose function is leadership to be the learners-in-chief. Our situation, then, is not hopeful. Once again we feel ourselves back at the very beginning, asking the same old question, "What more can I do?"

But it is not quite the same old question. The difference is that we are asking it not for children but for ourselves. It is our learning that is being limited, and hence our teaching. We are asking not, "What more can I do for children?" but, "What more can I do for myself?" We understand that the answer is the same as before. We have to learn what to do. And again we do not know what it is that we have to learn, only that to survive we have to learn what to do.

We may reflect for a moment how curious it is that the old question and its answer are repeated. If this simplicity is disconcerting, we may yet take courage from the fact that we have several times now acquired the necessary learning. Each time we tried to understand where we were so that we could find a place to begin. And if we have courage, we can do it again, now.

First, let us try to identify our task. If we can concentrate our energies on that, we may come to see how the peripheral difficulties can be dealt with. If we try to solve them first, we shall never get our task done, for the difficulties will then become the task. Let us forget then, for a while, our predicament with the school official and return to the class, to the responsibilities which we know are ours.

We have just come through the experience of the third lesson, and from it we understand that learning in the class is not dependent upon the curriculum, nor upon methods, but that it is in some way a natural process which is taking place within a framework, a habitat, as we have called it. What we have done is to release learning energies and to get individuals started on their own learning tasks, each taking a unique direction, but living within the framework. This state of affairs applies to one portion of the school day. Our task as a teacher is to maximize the learning of students. Clearly, then, we have to find a way in which the learning energy can be applied for a greater proportion of the school day.

We have already set a precedent for this. You will remember that after lesson one it became necessary to have more work surfaces in the room, and that during the following morning children who had finished their regular work assignments were employed to make tables out of cardboard boxes. Obviously, as a result of our afternoon activities, there will always be plenty of time fillers for the morning. The real challenge is in finding a way of using the basic studies program itself. Our problem is how to use the existing system. The generality of our task is clear. Let us then look at the demands of tomorrow morning when we are expected to teach.

Reading is first on the agenda. For this there would normally be four groups, each with a set text and an assignment to be worked on. The teacher would be with one group to hear each child read, while others followed the reading until called on by the teacher. At intervals the teacher would test comprehension by asking the meanings of words and phrases and by asking questions about the plot. In the other groups each child would read the text and afterwards answer the comprehension exercises at the end. That is the norm. Faced with this format, many teachers will ask again the old question, "What more can I do?"

In lesson three at least one group of children gives us the beginnings of an answer, the race track group. One of them remembered seeing a map of Le Mans in a book in the library. One book is not easily shared among six boys, at least for reading purposes! But the one book is almost an end product of their experiences, separately and together in the three lessons. There must be other books which they would find useful. Clearly, it would be best if the children could find their own, but given the restrictions of library hours and our purpose in borrowing, for a basic studies program, we are going to have to make the decision ourselves.

Let us think back on the way the group came into being. Michael cooperated in lesson one with Ben, and their bridge collapsed. Michael was upset, especially when David laughed. It was David, though, who helped Michael remake the bridge. It was David also who wanted to go on with the activity at the end of lesson one and who suggested making roads. In lesson two it was David who proudly asserted that the road he had helped to build was the best. Michael, who had a car, joined up with David to make a second road.

Tony did not finish his bridge in the first lesson, but he certainly wanted to. It was he who volunteered to bring cars from home, and in the second lesson produced them. He worked with Marvin on road-making, and later these two joined David and Michael in the creation of a road network, with David exhibiting leadership in terms of ideas and skills in executing them.

Bill worked mostly alone and was concerned with getting the road in proportion with the car's dimensions.

Jimmy, a playful fellow, was interested in the roads for racing cars on them, and it was he who won the road-making race with his partner Joel. It was after this that Joel joined in the gas station venture, leaving Jimmy to play his game alone. It is not clear what Jimmy's role subsequently became, but when last heard of each member of the group was working with paper and pencil compiling lists of competitors and statistics related to racing. These lists were being created to sound plausible. No facts were involved, but at this point the children were seeking them.

For three lessons the children carried on virtually without facts about bridge-building and road construction and without racing statistics. Invention was for them a necessity. They now have a need to refine their inventions, to know the details. They want to have a map of Le Mans.

From all this we may begin to understand something about the kinds of books they need to consult. They are children, but they are not looking for childish books. They need the real thing.

Many teachers will find this conclusion absurd, for even if what children want is the detail and the complexity of facts on road construction, or whatever, none of them can read, at least not well enough for advanced books. But surely this is the old argument again. "They can't do areas, because they can't multiply." It is not the multiplication that interests children. It is not the reading that interests them either, in our present example. It is the facts they want. To get those they will read, not word for word, stumblingly, so that comprehension is all but lost, but in toto. "Here is the figure." "What is this all about?" "This means. . . ." "No, it doesn't. . . ." They will talk, read, argue, ask questions, read, argue again, read, and help each other toward understanding. And while they are doing this they will acquire a familiarity with books, so that never again will books seem frightening—as they so often are to those who have failed to comprehend the value of a book to them. Speech precedes reading, yet to listen to struggling readers is to hear children who sound as if they cannot speak. Familiarity with books is acquired by use. Reading does not precede usage. Rather, the reverse is the case. Yet so often the kinds of books from which children are expected to learn to read are useless. There is nothing in them for children to come to grips with, no content worthy of their inventiveness and understanding. A trivial book is worse than no book at all.

Let us return to our problem of trying to use the reading lesson. There are six boys, each of whom has shown a fairly specific interest:

Michael—in cooperating to get a job done.
David—in doing more, and doing well with respect to construction.
Tony—in materials and aids to construction.
Jimmy—in competition and the thrill of action and winning.
Bill—in accuracy and proper proportions.
Marvin—in cooperating with Michael as a partner.

This group is self-made, and while David has seemed often to lead, the fact is that the task of the group is associated with Jimmy's prime interests. Now it happens that David reads quite well, and Jimmy hardly at all. The others fall between these two in their reading skills, so that ordinarily for reading purposes these children would be in three different groups. To keep the natural group and give it a new function, reading, will most likely result in destruction of the group. The group grew with its functions and with its different kinds of leadership and other roles with respect to those functions. To impose a reading function is to create disharmony in the group. It is to do in fact what is normally done to a class for teaching purposes. The aim is the teacher's aim, to teach reading. We readily understand yet again how it is that much teaching is destructive. We are now quite familiar with the fact that the aims of the teacher are not at all the aims of the learner. It is clear, then, that if we want to capitalize on an interest in a particular book, we must be certain that we do not use that interest for our own purposes, for the teaching of reading. Yet that is what we want to do. That is what we want to do because we are teachers. But we have learned, and we need to go on learning that the solution to our dilemma lies in the fact of our actions as students, as learners. Our aim will not be to teach reading. Our aim must be to learn—but to learn what?

Again, following our well-tried example, let us try to see where we are. There are six boys who comprise a self-made, natural group. They have been trying to compile the statistics of the Le Mans twenty-four hour road race and want to see a map of the circuit in a library book. We want to improve their reading skills and to use a regularly scheduled reading time for this purpose. To preserve the group in its present state of learning readiness we cannot allow it to become a reading group, nor to think of itself in this way. What we can do is to ransack the library for books containing information on bridges, bridge building, roads, road building, cars and car racing, and to find also the book with the map of Le Mans. These can be supplemented with motor-sports magazines. About twelve items will be needed for the group of six. At the beginning of the reading period the regular groups will form, and the teacher might ask the six by name to join her at the appropriate work area, the one used by the afternoon group.

"Here is the Le Mans map and few other books you might find useful." The options are left with the children. The problem of what to do and how to do it is theirs.

This situation is easily planned, but its development is full of imponderables. We cannot know in advance what will be the result of breaking the reading ritual. The group may break up into smaller units because of the diversity of the books, or it may come closer together because it has been specifically brought together and recognized by authority. There may be resentment at leaving the regular order. For example, David, the best reader, is now working with Jimmy, the poorest reader. The reading syndrome may be so strong that in spite of their options the children do think of themselves as being in a new reading group. Also, we cannot know how the rest of the class will react. They too may resent the select group. They also may want special notice.

Because of all this it may well seem that the teacher is going to be overwhelmed by problems. Even this slight departure from the ritual is going to create more difficulties than it solves. Now we are not out to create difficulties for children or for ourselves as teachers unless those difficulties produce the kinds of problems which will aid learning. What we have proposed seems as though it is going to promote resentment and hostility. These kinds of feelings do not help learning. It looks as though we have to abandon our proposal.

Surely, though, there must be some way we can create a workable situation. Maybe we are being too pessimistic about the chances of our proposal. Suppose we make one new group tomorrow, then another the next day, and so on, until the whole class enters new groupings formed on an interest basis. When put like this the disadvantages of the proposal become even more obvious. We are acting not as learners in the situation but as administrators, and we are doing what it is customary for administrators to do, making the changes bit by bit so that it will be easier for us, so that we can keep control. We are proposing to manipulate children! Far better for us to leave them with their present rituals.

The kind of change we are seeking cannot be effected bit by bit, slowly and gradually, simply because it is a totality we are trying to create, a habitat of which students and teachers are all a part. Lesson one exemplifies total change. There was nothing piecemeal about it. And our commitment in it was to learn, not to organize other people's learning.

What is our position now? Are we still thinking about six children and their desire for a book of facts? They were the clue that first started us thinking about this problem. From them we learned something about the kinds of books children want to read. Perhaps that gives us a new starting point, the books, the materials of mediation between the teaching and learning of reading.

We have twelve books in a group. Suppose we put other books into groups and then leave the children to go to the books. What we are now suggesting sounds like a library period. The children may well be interested in the books, but will they really read them? Surely they are more likely to look at them, then take another, then another, treating them with only superficial interest, just passing the time. What is their need to read? We have not provided them with any needs, which is what we conventionally would plan to do. They have none of the kind acquired by some of them in the three lessons. Now we are failing in motivation. This was never a problem for us before. Why suddenly has it become one?

Let us take a look at the situation. The prime elements are a group, books, and reading. We have lost our sense of the whole. There is no totality, no interaction, no interdependence. We need a habitat.

We got into this ridiculous position because we have been trying to use the basic studies program. We started with reading. We started with an element. But elements are not the basics in our new thinking, and so we have gone astray in our thoughts. If we cannot start with reading, it is equally unlikely that we shall be able to start with spelling, or with any other of the language arts. Can we, then, take language as a whole? Surely this should be possible, since communications, the bridging of the gap, was our former aim.

When we were first trying to understand how we might learn to communicate we played with words. It was thus that we found the gap to be bridged. It is obvious that at the moment we are really unable to know what it is we need to learn. We cannot readily define our problem. If we are tempted to give up, let us take courage from the fact that it is right now our learning we are concerned with, and that it is through our learning that we have come to promote learning among students. Let us, then, try to make a fresh statement about where we are, and play with it.

Language arts.

We want to enable children to speak, read, and write, to use language. We want them to delight in a mastery of words. Maybe they must play with words to learn, just as we are trying to play. Play with words.

Stupid?
Stupid!
Stupid story.
Extremely stupid story.
Extremely stupid story strongly stressing . . . strange street strollers?
Extremely stupid story strongly stressing struggling straggling strange street strollers.

Distressing!
Distressingly stupid! Never mind. Let's go on.

An ark in the park?
What a lark!
Mark you, . . .

Mark you,
Mark, you
You mark
You, mark
You mark my words. . . .

The rat sat on the mat.
Where are you cat?

Oh sad and wise,
With greenest eyes,
He dreamed of my demise,
Sighs.

Regard how hard . . .
The book he took . . .
His need indeed . . .
Approached a roach . . .
Wrong song.

Hey diddle diddle, the cat and the fiddle,
The boy leaped over the wall,
The little girl laughed to see such fun,
And the fuzz took off on a call.

A solution to pollution—dissolve it.
Examination of inflation—marks up.

Mary, contrary,
Wendy, bendy,
June, in tune,
Jim, the slim,
Gordon, Jordan,
Allan, a gallon.

She fussed, he cussed,
They missed the bus.

She sighed, she sat, she stood, she stared,
she sang, she shopped, she shouted,
she shrieked, she sewed, she squeaked,
she swept, she slept.

We have been playing, having fun with words, inventing meanings, withholding meanings, twisting and changing usage. We have the beginnings of stories, poems, reports, statements. We have the beginnings. There is speaking and reading and speaking again. Can we create something that needs to be spoken and read and written and spoken again and discussed and distorted and straightened out and added to and refined and carved up and put together? Can we use language as a material?

Many teachers will be disconcerted by—and even contemptuous of—the "stupid story." But if we think for a moment, it is the kind of experience that appeals to children—the cartoon—and allied with it the world of make-believe, of monsters and fairies, goodies and badies, and magic and mystery. In our first learning experience we saw the import of mystery. Reading is mystifying for the nonreader, a kind of black magic. It is, unfortunately, not a mystery, not something to be sought after and solved. Words in school lose their mystery. They become unidimensional symbols on a page, often devoid of meaning, even literal meaning. To learn the mystery of words and the arts of language, the teacher has somehow to restore the mystery, to recreate the complexity, and to make available the diversity of meanings and levels of symbolism inherent in language. If reading enrichment means anything, it surely must mean this.

It does not matter if we do not understand what children understand from cartoons, at least for our present purposes. It is sufficient that they derive satisfaction and delight from them. Visual and verbal imagery alike are distorted from the literary norms which teachers are trying to teach. If we can take the norm and play with it, elaborate it, distort it, so that it becomes a caricature of itself, a cartoon, we know that many levels of understanding will be achieved, or available for learning. Words will not then be unidimensional, belonging only to the comprehension of the teacher, the teacher's norm.

All this suggests, perhaps, that the teacher needs to be skilled in creating cartoons, or at least needs the ability to write a fairy story. It would certainly be useful, but it certainly isn't necessary any more than it was necessary for the teacher to be a bridge builder or a town planner. The teacher needs only to be a student, a beginning writer of children's stories, a beginning poet, a beginning lover of language. If the teacher can begin, so also will the children, and having begun, they will find their own way, not the teacher's way.

We may understand, then, that the "stupid story" is a beginning. It is a symbol for our learning, and not, therefore, to be understood by us as stupid. We are not poets, we are not skilled in the art of creating with words, and what we begin may always seem to us inadequate, unworthy of great language. It is somehow assumed that we should already have learned, that if we are teachers we should already know. But this is not so. We now know well enough that it is not necessary for us to be a master architect to teach building. Our task is to enable children to learn to learn, to love learning and to revel in its mastery. To do this we must be the chief learner. That is all.

Once we understand that we have to provide for a beginning. It is really quite easy to begin. There is the class. There is the teacher.

"Hi! Here is a list of H words: *happy, Harry, house.*" More words are called out: *hammer, happening, head, high, hit, hard.*

TEACHER: Let me see, Happy Harry hit his head hard with a hammer. . . ."

JIMMY: A happening, it's a happening.

TEACHER: So it is. A happening. Happy Harry hit his head. . . .

Eventually it turns out that "Happy Harry hopped high over a house, happening to hit his head hard on a hammer he had with him."

TEACHER: This is silly story number one.

JIMMY: That's a knockout! (*Pause for laughter*)

TEACHER: Oh Jimmy, you're so absolutely right! How about this: Knock, K-nock, K-night, K-not. Let's write a list of queer K's.

The story becomes, "The knock-kneed knight knotted a knitted kerchief round his neck" (silly story number two).

Soon several children start compiling their own versions, and, of course, desks get moved to enable new natural groupings to be formed. The teacher makes available colored paper and felt pens so that completed silly stories can be made into wall mounts suitably illustrated with pictures of Happy Harry and the knock-kneed knight.

Once groups have become established in this way each one comes to have its own peculiar needs and its own peculiar silliness. Very soon the free flow of conversation about words generates word associations, often out of reach of the teacher, unless she is an avid viewer of children's television shows. Monsters come early upon the scene, then dinosaurs and Batman and a host of cartoon creations. This is a very familiar world for most children. It is not without rules, though, for the paradox is that silliness has to make sense. And this is true also for the works of silliness that the children create, first in their speech and then in their attempts to translate this into the written word. Thus it is that punctuation has to be learned. It becomes, from the child's point of view, a necessity. The same is true with spelling and grammatical construction. It's no fun if you can't get it right.

GARY: This is the Land of the Dunderheads. This is a castle.

NEAL: Here comes Lord Dunderhead.

MYRA: He's wearing dungarees.

NEAL: Don't be silly. They're dundarees.

MYRA: And Lady Dunderhead has a dunderdress.

NEAL: Oh, you're so funny.

But they all laugh. The teacher shows them in an atlas a map of Scotland and points to Dundee. The group decides to draw its own map of Dunderland and starts to name some of the places: Dunder Headland, Dunderdown Hills, Dunderdrought Beach, Dunder Headsman's House, Dunderheadless Cemetery, Dunderhood Garage. Another group, also working with an atlas, is attempting to make up a Land of Spelling Bees, using real place names for invented places: Belle Island, Baffin Land, Bridgeport, Beaufort Sea, Belfort Gap. A search for specialized words is going on in another group of children who are trying to rename their neighborhood. They are using a dictionary and have so far come up with: Noisy Newtown, Pollution

Plaza, Petroleum River, Cancer Causeway, Trash Streets 1 through 10, Rat Roads 1 through 10, Butcher Block, Garbage Gardens.

Lists like the one just given are not made in a moment. Often they grow during the course of several days and go through many revisions. The list is a product of understanding at many levels. It is an expression of creativeness, of wit and humor, of social purpose and social conscience, and behind all this there is often the real-life experience which perhaps for the first time is being put into words. The children are not simply playing with words. They are using the arts of language.

These kinds of lists are obviously very different from the regular spelling lists. The words are usually more difficult, are usually correctly spelled (or correctly misspelled), always have an intellectual content, and are created by children in the process of learning. Other children appreciate the lists, and everyone has fun trying to extend them.

Once begun, the naming game has no end of variations, and it is rapidly developed beyond the listing stage and the silly story. Some children become very serious about the content of their work. What may begin as a playful poem, for example, can turn into a thoughtful essay: "The sky is brown, downtown. Mary made this poem, I wrote it down. We like blue sky. Most poems have blue sky. . . ." Behind the simplest looking story may hide a powerful intelligence: "I was mad. I told my friend. My girl she has it all. She can't have the earth." The teacher didn't understand this story until Arlene explained that her mother had told her to stop asking for the moon. Examples proliferate, as we should expect, for here is another explosion of learning.

This experience has shown us what it was hard to see in the three lessons—that there are no longer any lessons being taught! Children have been learning lessons in the sense that they have been learning to speak, to read, and to write. They have been learning phonics, sentence construction, punctuation, and all the rest, but the teacher, except perhaps for her introduction of Happy Harry, has abandoned any semblance of lesson procedures. Perhaps, as in the three lessons, a plan might be made in retrospect, or several plans, to cover all the different language arts, but we have got now to a stage where things are becoming too complex. The totality has to stand.

When we began thinking about language arts we were well

aware that the teacher would soon be called upon to explain her procedures. If we cannot find a way through this difficulty soon, the teacher is going to be in serious trouble, which hardly seems fair recompense for her achievements, but that is a fact of a teacher's life. This fact we are willing to face.

CHAPTER EIGHT

School Without Classes

It is no longer possible for the teacher to keep secret the work of her class—even if she wanted it that way—and so we now have to face the reality of a confrontation with the principal or other school officer.

Let's be clear about how we stand. We want to continue to explore learning with children. We have in the classroom a mass of new materials derived from our learning together thus far. These show without question that the achievements of children go far beyond the norm. We have evidence to back our faith in what we are doing. We need now to make that evidence public.

What we have done in the classroom so far has been private from the rest of the school, and for obvious reasons, but our survival depends upon our ability to become public. Our own learning in the classroom was public to the children, and now we have to see that the habitat in which we and the children have been working becomes a greater totality and incorporates what has to become the larger learning community.

In our public relations we are not aiming to sell an idea, a new way of teaching. To do this would be to invite judgment, and we would be judged not in our new terms but by the criteria of existing conventions. The outcome would be our demise. It would not matter that we could demonstrate all that the children had learned. The fact is that our classroom is messy and muddlesome and our class is talkative. It has living qualities which cannot be tolerated in proximity to the conventional pattern of law and order. It is plainly disruptive of the old order.

Our public relations, then, must be of a different kind. We must involve school officials, parents, and the community in the actual functioning of our public relations. In this way confrontation will be avoided. Again we perceive that the creation of totality cannot be a gradual, piecemeal operation. Essentially we have established in our class a system which cannot be subordinated to the existing system. Either we grow or we perish. We must take over or move out.

These are harsh words. We are teachers, not administrators. We belong in the classroom. We have no right to the take-over ambition. We did not bargain for this position at all. So far we have been content to use the present system, bucking it when we can, trying always to do a better job. But now it appears that we are being asked to perform a function for which we are wholly unsuited by temperament and training. We are asked to launch a publicity campaign to change the face of education. Ridiculous! If this is the answer to our original question, "What more can I do?" then we should have answered, "Nothing," and been content to follow the well-trodden way.

So some teachers will argue. They are angry, dismayed, frightened. Some fear to go back, and yet seem unable to go on. But we have met this situation before, and we know that when we are concerned with our learning we become better teachers. Let us see, then, how we may face this situation.

It is time for us to make a public declaration of our activities. We need to incorporate into our activities people whose function it is to judge us, so that if they do judge us it will be from an interior frame of reference. It is our hope, though, that when they come to operate in the learning situation itself their judgmental function will lose its relevance.

The activities of the class turn primarily on the arts of language and communication, and it is these arts which are to be made public. At this point we come to see that what looks like the curriculum, that is, language arts, is also the method that can aid us in our publicity objective. We have achieved a sense of totality in what were formerly, in the conventional teaching model, three disparate elements—curriculum, method, and aim. The unity comes about simply because we are concerned to learn. But the unity described here is only academic. It lacks a population. True, we have achieved the sense of totality, but never must we be fooled into thinking that the new habitat has been created until it is inhabited. This, then, is our problem.

In the classroom we do not have this problem. The curriculum guide advises teachers to go through exercises in spelling, followed by testing; sentence structure, followed by testing; the use of punctuation, followed by testing; and so on. All these activities are going on in the classroom as incidentals to the main function of teaching and learning—the creation of works of language using the arts of language. The functioning takes place through language, the means of communication between learners learning. They, the learners, are central to the elaboration of "silliness."

In a sense what we want to do is a piece of silliness. We have broken all the rules and now we want to publicize the fact. But like the children with their silliness our rule-breaking has its rules, and it is these new rules we want our public to learn. To do this they too will have to break rules—their own. Rule-breaking has to become legitimate. If we could launch "The Silly Season," or whatever we may wish to call our comedy of errors, then indeed rule-breaking would become the rule.

Suddenly our publicity campaign takes on the aspect of a performance. We need to advertise. We shall perform first to the school, during assembly, and later, but not much later, to parents, visitors, other children, the community. Obviously we shall need the help of school administrators. But let it be clearly known that ours is a comedy of errors and that the errors, that is, our departures from the conventions, are comic: the debasement, for example, of the standards of beauty set for school bulletin boards. It is "The Silly Season." It is our silliness that is being publicized and our fun in making it. Anyone can join and many will. In "The Silly Season" it is right for the hierarchy to step down. Thus is the new habitat born.

If we consider the ways in which the hierarchy may come to

cooperate, may come to learn how to be silly, how to play with language, and maybe how to play with children, we see that their learning is of a different kind from ours and from the children's, and yet it is part of the new habitat, part of the totality. We understand "The Silly Season" at many different levels. It is our new metaphor, disguising old rituals.

The decision is made. We have found a new direction. No time must be lost in advertising what we are about. Our survival depends upon the swiftness with which we can become public. We already have a mass of material awaiting exhibition. Some of it may not look presentable, but it is inventive and amusing and thus fits "The Silly Season" well. Mistakes, of whatever kind, will be the errors of comedy. They can be laughed at and forgiven.

In most schools it is something of a chore for the teacher to "do" the bulletin boards in the hallways, and for a teacher to volunteer for this job is rare indeed. We should have no problem in acquiring advertising space.

Once it is established that there will be a performance of "The Silly Season," the work of the class takes on a new aspect. The performance begins immediately, in the classroom. The exploration of language began with words, and the performance begins likewise. The teacher takes the "stage" and begins:

"Words, words, words, words. There are A words and B words and C words and magic words and funny words and queer words and silly words. Words, words, words, words. Here is silly story number one." The teacher pauses. Jimmy stands up and recounts the tale of "Happy Harry." It is not long before many contributions are ordered into a sequence. Sometimes there are gaps. Children understand not only that there is a gap but also they see how to fill it and understand what more needs to be created. They begin to see, too, the possibilities of playing with the gaps, the discontinuities. Always they are critical of their work and are constantly seeking to improve it. The children are all the time learning to help one another and the teacher. The skills of giving and receiving and the art of conversation are becoming well-defined features of the learning process.

KEVIN: Couldn't I be a driver taking some people from the airport?

STEVE: To center city? Yeah. Tell the people about it.

TEACHER: The passengers? See how it goes.

KEVIN: "Welcome to Noisy Newtown, I'm going to tell you the places of interest. We are driving by Petroleum River. It's a beautiful blue-green color. It smells so . . ."

SUSAN: Ucky.

VALERIE: Say, "It smells!"

KEVIN: It stinks! What comes next?

STEVE: Cancer Causeway.

KEVIN: Oh yes. "Here is Cancer Causeway, just right for smokers."

TEACHER: How about "ideal for smokers"?

KEVIN: What's that mean?

TEACHER: Well, it means just right.

KEVIN: That's what I said.

TEACHER: Yes.

STEVE: It's not right like this.

TEACHER: I don't understand.

STEVE: Well, its not funny anymore.

VALERIE: We could just read the list like, "I come from a real cute town. Oh, Noisy Newtown, do I love you! There's Pollution Plaza . . ."

Valerie gets all excited, goes into an impromptu comic routine, and gets a round of applause.

Two or three days go by. The children practice their "parts" at home, not because this is homework but because there is no way to stop them! This is what they want to do. Work and play are suddenly the same thing.

In Chapter Four we were concerned to find some equivalent in the classroom for the kinds of play children learn from outside of school. It seems that we are seeing now a reversal. Children are working at home with what they have played with in school. This is not the first time that children have continued their school-initiated activities out of school, but it is the first time so many of them have done so. We have never been overly concerned to make school work relevant, because operating with beginnings rather than endings, relevancy has not been a problem for the teacher. When children of their own volition start to work at home, then the work task is obviously independent of the place. It is relevant everywhere, every place the child is; otherwise the child would not be concerned with it. The work task has become also the means by which the school and the home become linked for the child. Another gap had been bridged. Education is opening up opportunities for the child's learning activities to be everywhere. This is precisely what education ought to do— but there is more. Opportunities are opened up not only for the child but also for his family and friends. What is fun at school becomes also fun at home. It becomes shared. It becomes public.

We were concerned previously not to limit our own learning opportunities to the patterns of the infant school and the integrated day program. We have here the first indication that more than openness at school is involved in what we are doing. Our own opportunities as teachers grow as our classrooms open up. The opportunities for parent involvement are becoming clearer. Best of all, what is happening to the child and for the child is not hidden from anyone, least of all the child! Let us continue in this direction toward what looks like the beginning of truly open education.

When children work at home other children become involved, brothers, sisters, and friends. They join the fun and make suggestions and additions, and the original version of the work may well change overnight. This situation is somewhat disconcerting for the teacher, and there are some interesting consequences. The teacher is asked if other children can join the show. They may be more talented in some respect, or they may have become a necessary part of a particular piece. This kind of merger produces a difficulty for the teacher, because what had started out as a class effort can suddenly no longer be regarded as that. Overnight the class unity has become obsolete in fact and a nuisance administratively. It is still there, but the whole cast for the performance is not. On a larger scale we are now seeing what has already happened within the class. Once children start a particular work task they form self-selected groups. Hitherto the task has been identified with a place, the classroom. Now the task is a performance, or rather the preparation for it, to be given, in a public place, so that the self-selected groups cut across the boundaries of the class place, and hence of the class. Either we think of the class as having grown (perhaps as not being large enough!), or, since it no longer conforms to the conventional criteria of a class, that it has ceased to be, temporarily at least. If the request for additional cast members were limited to an isolated instance, then the teacher might decide to hold the boundary conditions of the class and rule out other children. But once "The Silly Season" starts to become public, it is very hard to prevent people from joining in. The teacher is caught between the administrative unit and the functional unit. It is clear that the administrative unit if held gets in the way of the function, the task of performance for which learning is necessary. If the performance is to succeed, and if the learning is to continue, the teacher has to find a way out of this difficulty.

In most schools the lunch period is the only time in the day when people from different classes can meet without interfering with regular class schedules. Even meeting at this time may pose problems in schools where children go home for lunch or where the lunch period is staggered. In any event, the teacher finds herself working overtime. The only person who can make the necessary adjustments is the school administrator. Of course, the teacher can use the lunch period, but if some other arrangement can be made, then obviously there will be practical advantages. However, a precedent for future requests will have been set. The initiative will still be with the teacher.

When children from other classes begin to be involved in "The Silly Season," they will produce some slight changes within their own classrooms. These changes may not be enough to change outward procedures, but the skilled teacher will be alerted to the undercurrent of excitement. That teacher will also have noticed the advertising and may well want to know more about what's going on.

When teachers get together to talk there will be some kindred spirits. The talk will be about the fact that the children have come together and want to do something, and some suggestions will be made about how the children can meet during certain periods of the day. This, inevitably, will not include all would-be participants, but it is a beginning. "The Silly Season" teacher is, of course, the prime mover of this conversation.

Interestingly, what has just taken place is a further indication of an opening up. Lunchroom talk is no longer one long complaint. One teacher knows what more she can do, and she is doing it. Release learning energies in one place in the school and their effects will become known everywhere.

The teacher can now actively seek the help of the school administrator. The performance will be for the school, the parents, and the community, and thus the principal, on behalf of the school, can, in public, take credit for the performance. This is the teacher's ace. It is to the advantage of the school administration to encourage the performance and ensure its success. The teacher, of course, will need to have rehearsals in the auditorium. It is school business and important for public relations, so these can take place during school hours. The teacher has already consulted with other faculty members and knows which hours to choose. From the principal's point of view she has planned well, and that means a minimum of disruption for the school and for the administration. The teacher acknowledges that the performance is an outgrowth of language arts studies and shows examples of written work as evidence. The teacher reinforces the idea the administration already has—that she is competent, well organized, and so forth. It is vital that the administration have the assurance that the teacher knows what she is doing and that she is doing her job. There will then be no question concerning the peculiar classroom procedures which will be brought to their notice. The teacher keeps the initiative. She will, of course, ask for help and advice in the publicity campaign. It is important that the administration play a part in this function. The children have already prepared leaflets to hand out and would like to duplicate them. Permission is given. Arrangements are made, too, for distribution.

We understand what is going on in quite a different way from the administration, the rest of the faculty, and even the children. Our aim is not the same as theirs. For us the performance is not an end but a means, and thus we need to consider the aftermath of the performance.

"The Silly Season" came about because of our need for publicity. We needed to find some way of making it possible for the authorities in the school, the administration, to find out what we were doing and approve it. We needed the learning of the class to be made public, to the school, to parents, and to the community, so that the approval itself was made public. Having made a massive contribution to the school and to the community, we have reached another critical point in our totality of learning. There is a need, from the administration's point of view, for the restoration of order, a return to the status quo, to regular lessons. This is precisely what we have to avoid. Our explosion of literary learning erupted with the destruction of lessons and with the dislocation of the class. To return to the formalities of a class and to a routine of spellings and spelling tests, sentences and capital letters, and reading for comprehension is unthinkable. Ways must be found to continue the play of language arts in their totality. We need to initiate the development of a new habitat. Happily it is right at hand.

We have just lived the high spots of comedy and are now faced with the possibility again of conflict with authority, which for us could mean professional suicide, a tragedy. Again a metaphor comes to our rescue. Let it not be our tragedy. Let tragedy stand in our place. Exit the silly season, enter the sad.

If this is a metaphor for our professional situation, it also serves for the children. They have been elated by their creativity, their learning, their exposition, and the recognition they have received as language artists and performers. They too must drop from the peak of performance into a vacuum, wondering what comes next. Time is needed for a new surge of creativity to be built up. Feelings meanwhile are adrift. This period of aimlessness in children doesn't last long, but the fact that it is there provides a pause into which the teacher can insert possibilities for a new era of construction. It is a pause for the play of feelings and intellect. Soon new leads will come and a new direction will be found. Having in mind the potential for tragedy contained in the situation, it is not difficult to see beginnings.

Continuing the performance theme, the teacher might, for example, take into the class a recording of a tragic performance, I Pagliacci, perhaps, or the story of the defeat of a champion boxer, or a film, Scott of the Antarctic. If these choices seem a little exotic, and we admit their appeal is for the upper grades, we may reflect upon their relevance in these ways. The children have just been performers themselves, so they are more susceptible to identification with performers than would normally be the case. They know their performance was a success, and thus the tragic element will be in sharp contrast with their own feelings about their performances. With this contrast in mind their feelings will search around to find new direction. The contrast emphasizes—reinforces, perhaps—the vacuum in which they now are, so that they have to move again, the first step to new learning. The examples explore aspects of the human predicament. The developing habitat must have in it the great human mysteries if it is to grow to epic proportions.

Our aspirations right now may not be for the lofty heights of epic grandeur. Instead, we may feel very much the need for the mundane, the everyday, the ordinary. We do not feel heroic. As initiators of the new habitat in which we too have to live, we had far better turn the way our feelings tell us. The local newspaper carries a report of two children killed in a fire. It carries the bare facts, nothing about feelings. Is this sufficient material from which to build a habitat? There is the story; there are flames, smoke, suffocation, fear, dreams, nightmares, dark, terror. There is the story; there are the children, me and my brother playing with matches, secretly; guilt, crime, punishment. There is the story; my sisters, burned, good riddance, secret delight, public sorrow, hatred. The mundane begins to look alarming. Maybe the epic is needed in order to mediate private fears in public. Maybe this is what performance does.

But surely a simple story could not be so devastating. During Safety Week most teachers tell this kind of story. It has a moral. Interestingly, this is how many teachers keep order, by being a threat, by creating or using guilt feelings, by teaching the undercurrents of the simple story. With clear conscience they can deny this. It is only a simple story. The trouble with the story is its simplicity. No feelings are expressed, hence there is every place for us to project our own feelings and for children to project theirs.

If we take the simple story it looks as though we are in danger of creating problems which will hinder learning, or at least make it very difficult in ways hard for us to help. But we still feel the need to be down to earth. We are not ready for epic adventure. Yet to initiate a habitat it is clear that there must be an inherent complexity which both intellect and feelings can explore, where an individual need not be trapped by the limitations of individual experience, by overriding fears or fantasies.

The central feature of the simple story is the fire. The death is the incident, incidental to the fire. It is not embellished by associative feelings, and therefore it has no depth. The incident is unidimensional. It has no inherent totality. But fire, that is different. Suppose we take fire as a theme. Suppose we create a fire in the classroom, that is, we light a candle. This is the starting point. If we watch and listen, children's conversation will guide us in the ways we need to go. The lighting of a candle may signify a religious experience, the season of goodwill and festivities, the making of light, the making of dark, candle power, a poem. For the teacher all such associations are appropriate to the creation of a new habitat. In terms of preparation the teacher needs to have an assemblage of contingency materials which can become immediately available as the need arises.

It may be that this last example will turn out to be primarily a scientific investigation rather than a literary one, and for teachers who are still very much concerned to operate within the basic studies program, a more definitive beginning is needed. Our theme is tragic. We want children to read, write, discuss, argue about, define, relate to, and relate the forms of sadness. We must therefore provide them with the forms. They need a hundred pictures and more. How can the teacher get these overnight? Lack of materials would once have been an objection, perhaps, but no longer, since we are now able to incorporate children into the planning activities. They will help produce the materials needed for their learning activities. We have in the class a pile of old newspapers and magazines. These can be handed out with instructions to cut out sad faces. The pictures will need to be mounted. In a half an hour or so our materials will be ready.

"This is the face of sadness," says the teacher. "Look at the eyes. They are closed, they are open, they stare, they weep, they are red, they are bleary, they are wild, they dream. There are many faces of sadness. Sadness is many things."

Again some will wonder why the teacher does not ask, "What do the eyes look like?"

If it was our aim to have children solve a puzzle about the interpretation of facial characteristics, then perhaps the question would be in order, but it is not our purpose at this moment to have children come up with answers. To ask a question, to bring information to the fore, is to change the task and to destroy the kind of habitat we are trying to create. We want children to be thoughtful about a very large subject. We want them to feel, to express themselves, to verbalize. We do not want to challenge them to solve a puzzle, our puzzle. We want them to become informed of their own puzzles, their own feelings. We are trying to create a sympathy with sadness. We have our view and have expressed it. We have displayed our learning publicly and have thus provided a beginning.

It is clear that we can find a host of different beginnings, and once we have established one the development of the learning habitat proceeds apace. As soon as we are underway, then, the characteristic learning explosion takes place, and once again we have a mass of material. In less than a week there will be all kinds of written work. For some children this will consist of only a few lines; for others, whole stories. And all this material will be read, if only by its author. Reading, writing, talking—the totality of language arts—will be fully employed, unhindered by the limitations of lessons.

After our experiences with "The Silly Season" we know that there are other limitations which previously we had not suspected. These stem from the class unit itself. If the function groups include children of different ages and different backgrounds, even more work might be accomplished. The greater the range of experiences available, the greater also is the range of learning opportunity for every individual. We need to continue our own experiences in this direction. We have seen something of the learning potential of heterogeneous groups. Our job as teachers is to activate the potential, to maximize learning opportunity for children and for ourselves. Obviously, then, we need to extend the boundaries of our present habitat and again to establish public relations. Our reason for wanting publicity is now not merely for survival. It is basic to our future learning.

The school administrators, of course, will come to observe the return to normality. They will be met with masses of work, children's work, and the request for help with organizing the production of a magazine for circulation in the school and in the neighborhood. It scarcely matters whether this help is forthcoming or not. What does matter is that the work of the class becomes again public. It already, through performance, has exhibited itself, but what has to be made clear to the administration is that what happened was not simply a one-shot elaborate spectacle produced by an enthusiastic teacher but a continuing creative process by a group of children learning with their teacher.

The theme of the first issue of the magazine will be "The Face of Sadness," the metaphor we used for the tragic element in our professional situation. The fears of the administration were allayed by our first publicity campaign, but we have not returned to normal procedures and thus are still highly vulnerable. The publication of the magazine will restore confidence for a while and give us time to learn what more we can do for ourselves.

Additionally, to satisfy the administration, it will be necessary to give tests from time to time, but these, after the experiences of the class, will no longer be formidable and earnest affairs. Spellings can be quite amusing when they haven't been wrestled with for days on end. They are just words, and often their randomness and odd juxtapositions can be a source of fun to children who have been having fun with words. This is equally true for the teacher, who will soon find out that because of their greater experience with words the children find spelling tests much easier than formerly. Not only are the children relaxed in the presence of words, but they now have at their disposal possibilities for contrast and comparison which formerly was not the case. They have been playing with sounds, creating poetry, making the silly story. They will still make errors, of course. But that is part of being human. And we have only to show that the record is no worse than it was previously. It is likely that it will be considerably better, even after only a month of nonlessons.

As the magazine begins to take shape, children from other classes, particularly those who were involved in the performance, work informally and out of school, contributing, editing, and generally giving their help. In the class there is a sudden surge of interest to find out what magazines are all about; the children are not interested simply in their content but in their format, layout, and plan as well. In a very curious way the faces of sadness cut from magazines may now be the makings of the new magazine. Items are reformed and by this process the learners are informed.

The work that becomes available for the first issue will inevitably go beyond "The Faces of Sadness," and so even before a single publication there will be materials for a second issue. The work itself will open up further opportunities. What the performance began the magazine will continue indefinitely. In this sense there is a permanent link with the public. There is always a way of exhibiting the work of the class, and there is always a way open for others to join in. So far, however, this way is limited and relatively few can take part. Children have to be in other classes; adults perforce are out of school. The link is there, but primarily it is an outlet. There is publicity without much public involvement. Our links, our bridges, must involve two-way communication. Without it information has no living values.

We are still limited by the class unit. The class as a learning community is too limited in terms of age ranges, experience, and knowhow. The performance was particular to the class, but because of its place outside the classroom it enabled the breakdown into functional groups cutting across classes. The magazine is particular to the class too, but again, since it is distributed outside the class, there are marginal breaks across class barriers.

It is obvious that if we are to explore further we have to find some activity that can be generalized, one that will cut across class boundaries and not be dependent upon location in a classroom. If we are successfully to break down the notion of a class, we have to get out of the classroom.

CHAPTER NINE

School Without Classrooms

Our original question, "What more can I do?" is becoming progressively easier to answer. We have already found a great variety of answers and are prepared to look for more. We are presently faced with two problem areas about which we have to "do" something. First there are the limitations imposed on learning by the class unit itself. These we have uncovered as a result of our explorations in learning thus far. The second problem area is one of the conventional basic studies, namely, mathematics, which has not been directly discussed and which many teachers find difficult to deal with. We shall examine this latter area first, since its exploration may well provide possibilities for generalizing activities which cut across class boundaries.

Mathematics has its own conventions, its own structure. For most of us $2 + 2 = 4$. There is only one right answer. What happens when math becomes a part of some totality, a habitat, in which learners characteristically experiment and create? We have already seen the beginnings of an answer in the development of the three lessons. A variety of math activity—measuring; tabulating statistics; calculating speed, height, time, and distance; using scales and ratios—was necessary for working out tasks created by children. Mathematics was employed as part of a process. It was used as language is used. It was used as a language because it is a language. We have, then, a clue to help us find out how we may use the basic studies time allotment for math to maximize learning in this area too.

Recall, however, that the clue which started us off in our search with respect to language arts turned out to be somewhat misleading. Our mistake there was in trying to take what we had learned from the three lessons and directly apply it to the basic studies time for language arts. To avoid this kind of digression, then, we will leave what has become mathematically developed in the three lessons where it is and begin our thinking about learning math anew.

Many teachers may feel that this approach is unnecessary, since they already practice the New Math. Indeed, many of them will point out that though $2 + 2 = 4$, there are many ways in which this may be understood and written.

$$2 + 4 - 2 = 6 - 2$$
$$2 + 1 + 1 = 3 + 1$$
$$4 - 2 + 1 + 1 = (4 - 2) + 2, \quad \text{and so on.}$$

In this sense there is more than one right answer. These are the expressions of mathematical language. The importance of the New Math is that its emphasis is upon understanding and not upon mechanical manipulation. But our emphasis is not on understanding the New Math—nor indeed any other area of the curriculum—but very simply on learning. Our task now is to discover how we may use the time allotted to math for the purpose of learning.

When we were thinking about language arts we started by focusing on reading and came eventually to the conclusion that we needed to be concerned with the language arts as a whole. We played very simply with words and came up with the silly story. Let us see what comes of a similar play with mathematics.

Some teachers may shrink from this approach, not because they think it in any way illogical or ill conceived but because they shrink from mathematics, no matter what the approach. For them it is vital that they learn to begin again, that they learn to play. They will no doubt call up arguments like,

"I just can't do that with math."

"I'm no good at math."

"I don't have any math skills."

"It takes me all my time to deal with the New Math, and now you're asking us to play at math!"

"I'm no mathematician."

Almost certainly true! But then neither was that teacher a bridge-builder or a poet. The aim is, as always, for the teacher to learn. If the teacher can learn to play mathematically, then the children will also learn to play mathematically. Play!

Again some teachers will feel utterly lost: "What shall I play with?"

In language arts we played with the things of language—with words. Here, then, we must play with the things of mathematics, with numbers. Again some teachers will feel lost. Numbers can't come together to make a silly story. They have to be treated with respect. They are awesome. They are cold and remote. An obvious remedy is to humanize them. There is a growing dislike of being known by a number. Let's reverse the process. Let's take a number and give it human traits, that is give it a character. Taking the number 35 and adding the word "students," we signify the class. Adding one for the teacher, we describe us. We are 36.

> We are 36
> We have this many arms
> We have this many fingers
> This many socks, this many shoes
> Altogether we weigh ————————
> That's as heavy as ————————
> Altogether our height is ————
> That's as high as ————————

This is the beginning of our silly mathematical story. But where does all this lead? Even now, after all our other experiences, some teachers will feel that vague unease, because it appears as though there is no structure, and after all, mathematics *has* to have a structure. Let us continue.

There are 36 of us. How many things about us are susceptible to numeration? Our vital statistics—height, weight, age, sex—are obvious ones. Others might be pulse rate and temperature. We have enough for a beginning. Now our problem is how to create the conditions which will lead children to explore these kinds of numeration. They will need tools. If we give a child bathroom scales, he will immediately weigh himself. Give him a tape measure and he will measure anything and everything. Give him a stopwatch and he will start to time all kinds of activities. Given the tools, children will use them. Right away we begin to see again the possibility of a now familiar phenomenon, the explosion of learning. The initial activity will produce a plethora of data which need to be recorded and collated. The numbers are the raw material of mathematical learning. So, in addition to tools, we need record charts of some kind. We are playing at humanizing numbers, so why not list the names of all persons in the class to whom numbers will become attached. Lists of the names, carrying spaces to write numbers are distributed to the class. The tools and the materials are assembled. There remains the problem of organization, the initiation of the task.

Even now there will be some teachers who see the impossibilities of the situation rather than its possibilities. There is concern because the children cannot use a tape measure, do not know how to read off fractions of an inch, or even do not know that the basic unit is an inch.

Similarly, these teachers will argue, children are not able to read pounds, seconds, degrees, and so on. Here again is the now familiar argument: "But we can't do areas, because they can't multiply."

It is precisely because we want children to learn familiarity with pounds, inches, seconds, and the like that they need to measure. But the argument persists. "Well, at least let them practice with one thing at a time." This means let everyone use the tape measure or the scales or whatever. But this is precisely what we are trying to avoid. In order for relations to become established and harmonized, the complexities must be present. We associate mathematics with order and rigidity, and since we are not mathematicians, we find it virtually impossible to think about playing with numbers. We can't play with 8½. Neither can children. But 18½ seconds, 28½ inches, and 38½ pounds, these come to have meaning. That little bit, the fraction, gets to have real importance if it is the critical difference between you and someone else. Soon halves are differentiated into fourths and into eighths. Learning takes place at the margins.

We are already familiar with this idea. Ever since our first lesson children have been expanding boundaries, first by building the bridge and then the city and then by creating works for public performance. The conventional teacher, of course, acknowledges the importance of flexibility, in lesson planning, for example, so that the able child can go ahead, but flexibility is wholly inadequate to cope with a learning explosion. It is not that the boundaries must be made flexible but that new boundaries are ever being formed at the margins of the old. In mathematical terms this concept is perhaps easier to comprehend. It is implicit in the difference between understanding 7 and 8 and 8 and 8½.

The doubting teacher may perhaps be persuaded by the words, but still, how in the class will children come to know 8½ if they are not taught? It is this doubt that includes 8½ in the curriculum. It is the same doubt that engendered 20 spellings and the myths of history. Let us return to the 36.

The desks have on them a list of the 36. There are tape measures, rulers, yardsticks, bathroom scales, string. The children come in. They talk.

KEVIN: What are these for?

SUE: Look what I've got.

JOHN: Let me have a go with that.

VALERIE: It's 80 something.

SUSAN: It's 84.

KEVIN: Bet I weigh more.

TEACHER: Michael weighs 84 lbs.?

STEVE: What are those for?

MICHAEL: How d'you do that?

JOHN: Hold this end.

Everywhere groups are starting up. Children are copying one another, helping one another, competing with one another. The teacher may be confused, but most of the children are not.

A beginning has been made, and as with all other beginnings,

School Without Classrooms   119

once the initial step has been taken many of the conventional objections become irrelevant. The teacher will find herself assisting children to write down their findings, helping them on their insistence to find ways of measuring more accurately, discussing with them criteria for descriptive dimensions like arm's length and knee height.

In subsequent lessons data collected by individuals and groups will need to be made class property on massive wall charts and graphs. The walls become work surfaces. Information gaps will become apparent, and these will be filled. Statements will be made about what the graphs show and what they do not show. It is not long before children begin to see and to seek relations and to wonder about non-relations: "Do people with brown eyes weigh more than blue-eyed people?"

Very soon the children come to see that they need more people, and where better to find them than in the rest of the school? The counting craze is on, and once again the work of the class not only ceases to be bound by lessons but begins to operate outside the confines of the classroom. The class again becomes public. Again all this happens with startling suddenness. Learning explodes!

The problems now confronting the teacher may seem harder to deal with than those that had to do with language arts earlier. "The Silly Season" became a public performance. The counting craze does not lend itself to performance, but because our work has been made public before, and been publicly supported, we have advantages. There are sympathizers among the faculty who may well be prepared to join the fun, as they joined before in "The Silly Season." Obviously there are many ways in which teachers and classes can work cooperatively. They could be, for example, a simple exchange arrangement. A group from another class could come to lend themselves for measurement, and a group could go in exchange to measure an equivalent number in the other class. The teachers themselves might simply change places, the interested teacher to observe the work of the measuring class and the initiating teacher, perhaps with a small group of helpers from her own class, to start up the project in the second class. Or the classes might be amalgamated for a period, or some children might simply be borrowed from another class without any exchange. No matter how the meeting is arranged, there are bound to be two very important results. First, more data will be acquired, which will give rise to the need for even more. The results can hardly help but be puzzling. Second, the counting craze will infect more children, opening the way for other teachers to be more generous in their enthusiasm.

When two classes have become mathematically involved with each other their combined needs are for more and more people, the rest of the school. This may not be possible on a class-by-class basis, though others may well join. In any case the school officials must become involved again. The counting craze is well underway. There is lots of works to show for it. Let it show. Display it on the bulletin boards. Station children on corridors to do statistical counts. Enable children to interview classes on their favorite breakfast food. What are the favored colors this year for girls and for boys? Does this match the evidence as shown by dress? Is foot size related to height, weight, age, sex? What is a relation? Some children, and some teachers too, will begin to learn the excitement of the unanswerable question. When this happen the teacher will understand more clearly the value of questions and will be less likely to abuse them by ritual use as a teaching aid. The question and the quest are ways for learning.

Some teachers will find nothing mathematically new in all this. Nothing new is claimed in any curricular sense. In retrospect, as we are well aware, the curriculum area can be stated, the lesson can be worked out, and achievements detailed. What is new is the totality of the whole.

We are still so unused to thinking in terms of the totality of the whole that we cannot yet perhaps appreciate what our achievements have been. We can see that mathematically we have opened up an infinite number of possibilities, for the teacher and for the students, and that an immediate result of the work has been an unparalleled enthusiasm for playing with numbers. We can see, too, the direct results of teacher and class cooperation and know that the cooperation is genuine and friendly. It is not like team teaching. It is not like teaching at all. The cooperation is based upon an active participation in learning. These things we see. They are immediate and obvious. Associated with them is the growing sense of doing something worthwhile. It is shared by students and by teachers. There is a harmony of freedom and security, of doing right and doing well, of finding out and knowing the answers. School and work are suddenly fun things. Added to this are other developments, much less obvious, yet which lead to the opening up of an even greater range of learning opportunities. The math groups are like those which developed in the first three lessons and in "The Silly Season." They are self-selected, and characteristically they include students of varying mathematical ability. Faced with a workbook of mechanical examples, there would be some students who could do the problems, some who would, and some who couldn't and/or wouldn't. In the self-selected group, which also selects its specific task, all the members contribute. Johnny, who can't add with any certainty of being right, has no trouble measuring his height. He wants to be certain about it. So do his friends and his rivals. This kind of real motivation we are already quite familiar with, and indeed have come to expect and respect in the work of the self-selected groups. But we have added a new dimension to them when two or more classes begin to cooperate. The groups tend to become more heterogeneous. The age range is extended and with it abilities and understandings. The more diversified the groups become, the greater is the possibility for learning for everyone. It is easy to understand how younger children learn by being with older children. Most people can accept this. What is more difficult to understand is how younger children create learning opportunities for older children. Yet this is frequently what happens in the heterogeneous math group. Older children, because of their greater experience with math, begin to see possibilities beyond those of the less able or younger children in the group. As soon as an idea is comprehended, it begins to be suggested or explained, and there will be some in the group who do not follow. Now it is a self-selected group whose members are free to come and go and to express themselves within the group as they wish. Sometimes it happens that a quiet member who has not understood may get up to leave, or that the silence of that member, whether he makes a move to leave or not, provokes comment from the originator of the idea. He wants the group to understand. He is proud of the idea and starts to expound it again, and as all good teachers do, he tries to express it in a different and simpler way. Some more vociferous member of the group may interrupt or reinterpret or even alter the logic, and this produces renewed exposition until the originator of the idea has uncovered all the steps in the mathematical progression which he may at first have intuitively jumped. Thus his understanding becomes greatly elaborated and quite explicit because he has had to simplify his first version and to build it up from the beginning. In doing this a variety of calculating methods is sometimes discovered, as well as shortcut ways of computing.

The kinds of ideas generated in heterogeneous groups lead to a differentiation of the initial activity. The number craze will persist, but is likely to take on many different forms. Eventually the kinds of investigations will proceed beyond strictly mathematical bounds, and it may become impossible to designate them with a curricular label. Then another bridge will have been built. Ultimately it does not matter where the starting point has been, whether in social studies, in language arts, or in mathematics. Once a habitat has become established, then it is explored in its entirety. It is lived in, played with, described, written about, measured, discussed, argued over, knocked down, rebuilt, made habitable.

The "three-lesson" class has experienced this in full. Other classes are now joining in, and while children are quick to seize the new opportunities, it is still hard for their teachers to know how to handle what is clearly a difficult administrative situation. The public performance was fine for "The Silly Season." "The counting craze" was tolerated by the school officials. It didn't get in their way, and such an interest in math is pretty impressive. But now we have reached another critical stage. Math is developing, along with heterogeneous groups, new characteristics: it is becoming less easily identified with curriculum requirements. Diversity is becoming increasingly hard to handle in the language arts period, too. Other classes are trying out different kinds of social studies programs. Children are beginning to wander in and out of classrooms at all times of the day, and the fact is that they are usually on legitimate business.

For teachers committed to the new openness, a return to the old rigidities is unthinkable. For school administrators the situation is getting out of hand. They know what is going on, even if they don't know why. And they also suspect, because they have been well supplied with evidence by the teachers, that something is being learned by children. The test results are no worse—in fact, they are a bit better—and the students seem suddenly more interested. The bad ones haven't been sent down to the office for some time now.

It is clear that when this situation has been reached there is a need for a public demonstration of learning viability, and a public recognition of a new order within the school. The old conventions cannot live happily alongside the newly forming structures, simply because children and teachers alike cannot conform to a duality of behavior patterns. It is not possible both to go with the new group and stay in the old class. It is not possible to make choices within an order which makes none available. Hitherto the teachers may have been concerned to avoid change because it was not expected of them. Now that they have become involved in the change they have to create for their administrators a way in which change will be expected of them. And it must be done so that it will not interfere with the old order. Destruction may come to the old order, but destruction is not a virtue. We are concerned simply, as always, to create possibilities for learning. We do not wish to fight. That gets in the way of learning.

Inevitably, it seems, we return to our original question, "What more can I do?"

Almost as it is asked the beginnings of an answer come. It is really no longer "I" who am asking the question, but we, we who have been cooperating together, working and learning with children, first with math and now with a whole range of tasks. We are together. We want to remain together, to extend our contacts, to learn together new ways in which we can help children to learn together. We want to go on doing what we are doing. That is the answer. How is this possible? That is the question!

We are three teachers (or four or five). We need three adjacent rooms, as far as possible isolated from everyone else. We want a corridor or a floor or some physical unit so that we can operate as if we were a separate school. Then, our "school" rules could legitimately be different from the other "school." Getting agreement from the school administrators on a matter of this magnitude seems a formidable task. There are lots of arguments which favor its adoption, but even the most persuasive ones fail if there are harsh feelings. For such a venture to succeed, a great deal of goodwill is required on the part of the administration, as well as support from the rest of the faculty.

Let us consider some of the ways in which support may be gained. It is important that what has been done be public. The activities must not be viewed as subversive. Now it is true that in the beginning the three lessons began behind closed doors, but there was nothing dishonest about that. They were operated within the system. Soon afterwards the work in language arts was directed toward publicity. During the "counting craze," too, stress upon the openness of the activities was a necessity for the work task. Thus when the demand for an autonomous unit is made, the rest of the school is well aware of the kinds of things that have been going on. They may not approve; they may feel threatened, violated, or otherwise badly treated, but the activities in which we have engaged are open to their scrutiny. This is our protection. What we have done is not through spite or malice, and we have not sought to condemn conventional practices. It may seem this way, though, especially if it succeeds. In fact, it is our very success that creates the problems. The more it is seen that the students are learning and are wanting to learn, the greater is the discrepancy between the conventional order and the new developments. Moreover, from the standpoint of conventional order, the new developments look like disorder and are thus doubly threatening. But if we continue to do our task publicly, two things happen. First, the old order may wish to hide the new, to disown it, to get it out of the way, so that no comparison can be made and so that there is no interference. Thus when we have become established as a group of teachers, we can be effectively hidden away and thus be free to go on developing our new ways. Second, publicity forces recognition, and if there is success to be recognized, then some people will be prepared to back it whether they understand it or not. Both ways, the publicity works to our advantage.

Let us assume that the group of teachers committed to the new way are sufficiently strong in their support of one another as a group to persuade the administration that they want to explore more fully the advantages of cooperation and that they want to do it with a minimum of disruption to other faculty and the rest of the school. Obviously this latter argument needs to be put strongly, not as an excuse, not as an apology, but as a positive statement: simply, we do not wish to disturb you.

Clearly this move will not be easy, but it is possible, because administratively there are advantages. For us the advantages are educational, but our need for educational survival depends upon our being able to make our plan easy for the administration to administer. If we are all together in one place, then they know where we are! It looks as though we have what we wanted, too, namely, isolation. We shall understand this, though, as isolation from interference by others rather than an isolation from interfering with others.

School Without Classrooms

Once a bloc has been established, effectively there are two schools, perhaps sharing the same building. There will be points of contact, of course, such as the library and the auditorium, and it is in these places, the public places of the school, that the publicity must continue to flourish. The isolation is not to be thought of as an educational function. Its purpose for us is to guarantee some protection for our efforts to develop a new way of working, at least for a short period. We do not wish to set up new barriers in place of old, but learning takes time, and we need that time together as a group. We do not want to be sidetracked in our learning by having to battle against conventions which for us are inoperable.

Let us suppose that we have been successful in obtaining a corridor or some other unit of the building and that while we must still turn in test results at appropriate intervals, we do have considerable freedom to operate together. Naturally, we shall be expected to report on our activities. This we fully intend to, in detail, and as publicly as possible. This is our hope for continued survival. We need to be known.

The area allotted to the group comprises three rooms on the end of a corridor, with a staircase leading to an exit into the yard. There are three teachers and their three classes. It is the beginning of a new work period. So far the teachers have learned that curriculum requirements can be easily covered without making them the basis of daily routine, that formal lessons are not needed to regulate the daily increments of learning in subject matters, and that the class unit is not the same as a learning unit. Their purpose in coming together is to learn how to maximize learning possibilities for the students and for themselves. Once again we have the situation in which the chief task of the teacher is to learn, and we know from our experience that when the teacher learns, then the students learn too.

Once again the task may seem impossible. These teachers are still haunted by the old question, "What more can I do?" Once again the answer must be sought by trying to understand the situation we have arrived at.

Let us reiterate. There are three classes, three teachers, three rooms. There need be no set curriculum, no set lessons, no set teachers, no set students. There must be a framework in which all can work and which can grow as the work grows. There must be a habitat. The need is to create something, to make something. But what? In our previous attempts to find a solution to this kind of question our recourse has been play. We have only to find a beginning. Play.

We need to create something. We need to make something. Once we built a bridge to bridge something, a gap. Now we need to make in order to make something, a new way of learning. What kind of a thing could be made to make a new way of learning? Our metaphor is precarious. To find a place to begin we need something more solid, a foundation, perhaps. We feel insecure. Our career may be in the balance. We are committed irrevocably to finding a new way, and yet we doubt that we can. It takes courage to learn.

We want to feel secure.

We need something solid.

Our career is in the balance.

These are our thoughts. Can we find some activity which will give substance to these thoughts? Can we translate thought into action via metaphor, as we have done before? We feel we are in the balance. Suppose we made a balance. Suppose we took balance as a theme. Now we have something to work on. Maybe this will provide us with the kind of framework we are looking for.

Let us think first of all in terms of work tasks, the actual doing that will develop and be the means of our learning. The learning must always be what we think about first.

Suppose a string to be suspended from a high point, and suppose a drinking straw is attached to it a short way down, and then to this straw are attached two other strings, on either end, to which again are attached other straws or pieces of straws different in length from the first and from each other. We have the beginnings of a mobile, a delicate balance, of mathematical proportions and artistic skills.

Suppose a bead frame with 10 by 10 beads is arranged in many patterns and that these patterns are recorded by impressing the stub end of a pencil in damp clay or by gluing dried beans or peas on ten tongue depressors. There are many symmetrical patterns. Some child will say, "That is a Z."

Letters have a symmetry. They need to be balanced in juxtaposition, on a line, on a page. There are many forms of print. There will be a need to look at books, not for their content but for the way they are printed. The same applies for newspapers, magazines, posters, and ads. There will be a need to make prints, to stencil, to draw letters, to color them, to play with arrangements. Some have mirror images.

Suppose we play with mirrors and mirror images, with reflections, with simple cameras, with developing images, and let us look at pictures and make pictures.

Suppose there are pictures of fish, an octopus, sea urchins, and starfish. There is bilateral symmetry and radial symmetry. Living things have symmetry. Get a bag of bones and reconstruct a skeleton.

Suppose a crystal is grown,
A contra dance, a square dance,
A pile of blocks,
Puppets on a string,
Scales and equations,
Scales and justice,
Play in the park on swings and seesaws,
Suppose Humpty Dumpty and overbalance.

Suddenly we understand a whole new range of possibilities, balance and imbalance, symmetry and asymmetry, pattern. We have needed a new kind of order. Let us learn order to create order and make patterns which we can change and recreate. Our search for what to do is ended. How shall we start?

There are three teachers, each one having special knowledge and particular interests. It is easy, therefore, for them to select out of the many possibilities a few which interest them and which they wish to continue to explore. Once the whole is comprehended, it does not much matter where the beginning is made. We know from experience that a beginning has to be made right away by the learner. A speech of preparation by the teacher is likely to be an immediate embarrassment and disadvantage, even if it is short. Thus there must be put out materials which are immediately available for use, and where the explanation of usage, if it is not implicit in the materials, is made known by example. Then the conversation will start. Then the children will be able to state their problems, their hopes, and their wants. Ideas will be generated, independent of the teacher, who must listen in order to discover how to provide for further exploration. This we know, and we must not be tempted to do otherwise.

The problem now facing the three teachers is not what to do, nor probably how to start, but rather how to organize the children and the work spaces. The administration has to be made to fit the work task. We now begin to see more clearly than ever before, perhaps, why the conventional set-up is so hard to learn in. There the administration comes first and everything else is made to fit it—only learning won't, so it doesn't take place. The three teachers may feel at this point that they are not equal to the task. The trouble is that they have no precedent to go on. There is no pattern they can follow. All the time the pressure is on them to create.

Thus, there is no precedent, no pattern. Until the work has begun, it is hard to see what pattern will be useful and helpful. The immediate problem is really to get all three classes working so that the tasks they perform will begin to suggest the most useful kinds of groupings and timings. Since the whole reason for getting into this situation was so that the classes might work on a self-selected group basis, the notion of classes and of belonging to a class has to go. This can be achieved only if each child is freely allowed to select the place he will work in. This mean that a number of places must be available to him. Suppose two rooms are set out so that there are a number of works areas, separated perhaps by partitions, so that each area is an entity. In each entity there are specific materials available for four or five children to work at. There are no teachers' tables, and there is no space up front. The whole of each room is used, so that forty children can be accommodated in each of the two rooms. There are fewer chairs in the room than people. That is no problem. Not everyone is going to want to sit down at the same time. The grouping of the tables or desks means that even though there are more children in the rooms than would normally be the case, there is also more space and more room to work.

In the corridor other work areas are set up. These can be temporary affairs such as will not contravene fire regulations. A pole balanced between the tops of two chairs suffices to suspend three or four mobiles.

The three teachers are as free to choose their locations as the children. The doors will be open. The teachers will go where they find the need. They may choose to be with one kind of work task rather than another because they know more about it, or because they know less, and wish to learn.

The children will probably have been lined up outside with the rest of the school. One teacher will ask them to come in. As they arrive they may simply be asked to take a look around, then choose a place to work. The other teachers will already be working. They are working examples.

Soon after an expectably noisy initial period most children will get started on something. Others may need help and may even need to be assigned to a work area where a choice of materials is available and where two or three children may already have begun. There is still choice for them, but it is not so great that they panic and do nothing. Remember that these children have already spent time working with one another and that this kind of experience is not therefore entirely unfamiliar.

At the end of an hour much work will have been done. This must be displayed so that everyone can see how much the whole group can achieve and how different people have done different kinds of things. There must be possibilities for comparison and contrast, even for judgment: not this is bad or that is good, but this doesn't hang right, that is lopsided, and that is very pretty.

All this comes before the teacher's explanation. After the achievement there is something to look at, something to think about. Something is already known by everyone. Any explanation about what to do with finished articles, where to put spare materials, where to keep personal notebooks, and all the rest now makes some sense. New procedures are learned alongside the new patterns.

The third room has not yet been used. What we have done so far is to show that the other two rooms are open and available for everyone and that the corridor too is also a work area. The walls are physical barriers only, and if they could be taken away there would simply be more working space. We have arrived, then, at a situation where classrooms are no longer needed, because we no longer have classes. But there is the third room. It will come to have many purposes, but it is distinct from the rest. It too can be used at any time, by anyone who wishes to be quiet, to read, to write, to think, to sit, to be alone, to dream. Sometimes it will be used for small meetings. Sometimes everyone will crowd into it, to sit on the floor and listen to music or to make speeches or to grumble in public. It will also be the place where the television set is, where records are stored, where there are books not in immediate use, where there are office supplies, and the like. All things are available, always. It is not that they are hidden, only that they have their place. The three rooms are like a house where everyone lives, but where there are some special-purpose areas. Things have their places, not people. They have responsibilities.

We have arrived, then, at a situation where the internal walls of the school no longer hide and separate the activities within it. The walls may be there, architectural accidents in school design, but the notion of classroom has disappeared along with classes and lessons. These are being replaced by open spaces, open groups, open activities, open education, open-ended education.

There is one other aspect of our three-room–corridor school we have so far neglected. The corridor leads to a staircase and to an exit.

CHAPTER TEN

School Without Walls
or
Classes Without
a School

We have come to the exit. It will be no surprise, after all our other experiences, if we regard this doorway as yet another opening, an entrance to what we are still striving for, public education. Within the school our success and our survival have depended upon our public actions, our learning in public. The same is true without the school.

The immediate problem facing the three teachers is how to make that entrance, how to become public. Again our experiences will help us, for even in the early days of our learning the need to go outside the school for information, materials, expert help, and experience was obvious.

How wide is a river?
Please, Mr. Storekeeper, can we have cardboard cartons to make
    tables with?
How big is your car, Miss?
What happens to planes wanting to land when they can't use
    the runway?

In terms of need, or motivation, there are no problems. It is the contact that is difficult. In the conventional system children take trips. These are planned, often months in advance, and the whole class goes to view some historic site or to be escorted through a museum. Usually the students have a great time, even though most of them are not much awed by the exhibits. They are out of school and that alone is enough to excite them. Our needs are obviously very different. The historic site and the museum by definition exhibit the past, not the present—and certainly not the future—and except in quite specific individual instances are remote from the kinds of problems that children want and need to solve and the kinds of learning that will make it possible for them to survive.

It is true that in the conventional system children take trips to the airport or go for a boat ride around the harbor. These expeditions are fun, and children do learn from such experiences, but they are still remote from the kind of contact needed for public learning. The airport and the boat ride are treated as bits and pieces of the curriculum, as subject matters. In some way it is supposed that a knowledge of them will be conveyed to the students. To assist in the conveyance the teacher is there, and perhaps also an expert ready with facts and figures. Essentially we are back where we started. There are the two sides, the teachers and the children, and there is the body of knowledge to be transmitted. This was our position before the building of the bridge. It was not until after we had built the bridge, and explored the land on either side of it, and begun to build the city that we found ourselves in the middle of the explosion of learning. And even then for some there was a doubt that we were not really doing our job as teachers, that is, of transmitting, or conveying, a body of knowledge. It is perhaps only now that we can see how much our thinking has changed, so that we are no longer concerned with lessons and the curriculum and facts and figures and all the things that go to create what in conventional terms is assumed to be a body of knowledge. An airport means different things to different people. To the traveler it is one thing, to the pilot it is something else, and so too to the politician, the pollution-control expert, the customs officer, the taxi driver. It is something different again for the child who visits it. He has no real place there and can experience no interaction. He may wish to become a pilot, a customs officer, or a taxi driver in consequence of his visit, but his visit is not likely to help him do this, nor to give him the opportunity of finding out whether his choice is the right one for him. In the conventional system his learning is stopped at the very point where it begins. We saw this characteristic before in our early observations of classroom practice.

There is a further characteristic we should note about regular school trips. They are unilateral experiences. Children are exposed to an experience from which they are expected to learn, but there is no recognition that anyone may learn from the children. There is no way for children to make a contribution. It is not possible for children to be teachers in the experience. Having built our bridge and created two-way communication, and having learned to be a student with other students, we find ourselves unable to accept the procedures required for regular school trips. It is very clear that once again we have to learn new ways. We are students.

We left the three teachers in the process of building, with the children, a new habitat. Together they have been exploring balance, symmetry, and patterns, and they are trying also to establish among themselves ways of ordering their social relations. Some patterns have already become formalized. Places for personal property have become established. Children and teachers use notebooks like laboratory notebooks, to record, in numbers, in words, and by diagrams and illustrations, their day-to-day discoveries. Older children help younger children to do this and use their own work as illustration. Young children question older children and thus help the older children to assess and refine their own efforts. At the end of the morning and again at the end of the afternoon there is an "everybody" time when the children and the teachers meet to listen together, to talk together, to complain, or to laugh as a family. There is a real sense in which these activities become the the new conventions. The difference between these and the old-style conventions lies in the way they have come about and in the way they are susceptible to change as new needs arise. They are open to change. To protect this openness and to guard against ritualization, it is imperative that the final plunge into public life be taken. When once the educational process becomes the public thing, then its ritualization or socialization, its habits, are the habits of a people, of a whole society, not simply of a small, specialized, enclosed group of professional educators. Thus it becomes diversified, accountable, and responsible. It is truly open education.

With the three teachers working with the children who have formed themselves into a great number of groups we are witnessing another learning explosion.

PETER: Men move sideways, too.

MARY: It's sort of hard though, going like this.

FIONA: Not very fast they don't.

PETER: Yeah, but they can do it.

TEACHER: They don't often choose to. (*Pause*)

PETER: It'd be funny moving mostly sideways. Like being in space. Spacemen float about. That makes them move differently.

The conversation continues and it becomes apparent that the bilateral symmetry of man gives him advantages of movement in certain directions and that the same is true for many animals.

MARY: How about trees?

PETER: They don't move.

FIONA: Only when the wind blows.

MARY: I know they don't, only. . . .

TEACHER: Say some more.

MARY: Well, but they grow all round.

TEACHER: Um.

PETER: You mean growing all round is sort of, sort of. . . .

TEACHER: Like moving all round?

PETER: Yes.

MARY: Yes.

TEACHER: I never thought of that. As a matter of fact, I don't really know what a tree looks like—I mean, how it grows out.

MARY: We could take a look.

TEACHER: O.K. I'll come out at recess.

MARY: Why can't we go now?

Probably for the first time in her career the teacher has no reason for not going out. She has no class, no classroom, no schedule, no commitment except to maximize learning opportunity. At this point in time the only way to do that is to go and look at a tree.

Preliminary unscheduled excursions into the immediate neighborhood soon become an integral part of the work of the class. They are almost always made in order to answer particular problems of particular groups. Very soon the neighborhood people get used to seeing small groups of children measuring the distances between lamp posts, counting passing cars, interviewing a passer-by, or examining a pile of garbage. They stop to find out why. They start to talk. They start to participate. They start to teach. These people would never enter a school, except perhaps to complain to the principal about children's misdemeanors. It probably would never occur to them that they had anything to teach. And it would be equally unlikely that they would ever seriously think of listening to a group of children. And yet it is easy for them to join a group of children watching a man digging a hole. They laugh and joke together, and the man digging the hole gets to feel pretty important. He has a contribution to make. He is a teacher. But this can happen only when the group is not a horde, when it is a familiar neighborhood sight, and when it is friendly and obviously trying to learn something. Learning and teaching are both infectious in these circumstances.

Some teachers may find it necessary to object at this point that if classes were smaller, if there were more teachers, if the time schedule permitted, then they too could do these things. Probably they could not, because they have not built the bridge. But it is worth looking for a moment at what is clearly an administrative problem, namely, how to deal with large numbers. Technically, in the large group, the teacher-pupil ratio is 3:100, but, in fact, in open education the proportions are constantly changing. When the teacher goes off with the tree group, then the ratios are 1:3 and 2:97, though even these ratios do not reflect what is really happening educationally. In the tree group the teacher is going off to learn. There is no teacher. Among the 97, there will be a large proportion of students teaching others, and the two teachers will be giving their attention to only a few students at a time. This does not mean that additional teachers would not be helpful, only that given present teacher-student ratios, open education is a viable alternative. In fact, in administrative terms, personnel resources are more usefully employed. Absence of a teacher does not mean that a class is left with no teacher. It is not a disaster if no substitute arrives. Neither is it a disaster if a substitute does arrive. Essentially, we mean that given present facilities, without additional expenditure, there can come about a radical change in the meaning of school for the student and teacher alike. There can be a happier and educationally more productive alternative.

Once the opening up in public has begun, as we should expect, there occurs another explosion, an explosion of learning opportunities. The neighborhood grows in size. It is as though another bridge has been built and the land immediately about is explored. As it is explored, its resources are discovered.

When children, and teachers too, have become familiar with the idea that they can go outside to answer their questions, a number of changes occur of far-reaching consequence. Let us see what these are and how they come about by following up the episode of the tree. Peter, Mary, Fiona, and the teacher were talking about directions of movement in living things, and growth in trees was suggested as a kind of vegetable movement. The teacher knew nothing about how trees grow, and it was at Mary's prompting that the group went outside to look.

PETER: There's a tree.

FIONA: You can't see it grow.

TEACHER: You'd have to stand there a long time.

MARY: You could come every day and look.

TEACHER: I wonder what you'd look at, though.

PETER: We want something to measure with.

TEACHER: How do you mean?

PETER: Like a tape.

TEACHER: But what would you do with it?

PETER: Measure round it.

TEACHER: Round its trunk?

PETER: Yep.

MARY: You'd have to do it in the same place every day.

TEACHER: Suppose it's already a grown tree. Grown-ups don't grow.

FIONA: Get a little tree, then.

TEACHER: Maybe we need several trees of different sizes.

A lengthy discussion follows in which the idea of the growing up of trees and of people is explored. At first physical growth is the criterion, and then other aspects of growth are considered.

FIONA: Trees can't be bad.

PETER: They can be good.

TEACHER: How so?

PETER: Well, like for climbing.

TEACHER: But that means the tree is good for you, good for you to climb. That's different from the tree itself being good.

PETER: Yes. (*Pause*) I know a tree that looks good, though, but it's bad. It breaks.

TEACHER: It's not strong enough?

PETER: Yes. No. It falls to bits.

TEACHER: It's rotten.

PETER: Yeah. Rotten old tree.

TEACHER: Yes. That would be bad for climbing. But that doesn't mean the tree is bad, does it?

MARY: It's not good.

TEACHER: No.

MARY: Well.

TEACHER: Maybe we could say it was unhealthy.

The conversation dies down. A thoughtful silence falls on the group. The teacher is reluctant to pursue her own line of thinking. Disease and age may not be bad, and in trees they can be easily chopped out. In people. . . . The teacher suddenly feels lost. Open education can certainly lead to dangerous openings. The teacher feels unable to cope with moral issues. Is this, after all, a part of her job? Professionally she is expected to be nonpartisan. In the conventional class

School Without Walls or Classes Without a School

life and death issues can be avoided. They can be forbidden. They can be ignored. But now the rules are different. The teacher is trapped into honesty. That is part of the new habitat in which there is no hiding.

The teacher's moment of panic passes. After all, the children are not following the teacher's logic. But suppose they do. What kind of preparation, beyond honesty itself, does the teacher need to cope with such a situation?

In a very curious way schools have come to isolate themselves from moral issues, from concern with the way a man should live. Thus, when we begin to open up our education and start to live again, these issues suddenly spring up in front of us. The fact that they do indicates the success of our venture in open education, but it is a problem which has been excluded by educators for so long that it may become for many the new curriculum. Older students perceive this situation before their teachers. They know that the moral issues in school and out of school are at variance. They want to know how to live. They need to learn. They cannot do this in school.

Suddenly we become aware that while we may have thrown off the set of old problems by working outside the old conventions, we have encountered what may be a new set. Irrelevancy has been replaced by relevance, so that our task is now to deal with live issues. We have to deal with reality, not fantasy. Our task is educational because the solutions are and will be living solutions. Because they are living, they are in a state of constant change, and it is in this state that our learning goes on, by, with, and for. Such problems are not to be thought of as discouragements. They are the very means of learning. They are the necessities of life, and life cannot continue without their solution. Problems are constant.

If we can accept this, we begin to see another aspect, another opening out in educational thinking. In the old conventions a problem existed to be overcome. Once overcome that was the end. Thus at the beginning of a lesson a teacher could state an aim. The aim was the end—an end because often it was conceived as an end product that could be measured. The child was tested and his score recorded. This score itself was a finality—not to be changed, just added to, perhaps—a mark of achievement or of failure to be carried by the student throughout the course of his educational career, which also in the conventional system had an end. In our new thinking problems are incidents marking progress. They are the means not only through which learning may take place but also through which further problems may be sought. The problems make learning possible. If there were no problems, there could be no education, for all would be known.

Thus our new set of problems is not a cause for concern. They are truly educational problems. That is, they assist our education. That may be hard for the teacher. The problems exist outside the school. This is where we meet them. This is where we are at.

A whole new educational perspective opens up once we get outside the school, once education becomes public, once it becomes open. It is only in the school that men grow like trees.

We left our teacher concerned with her thoughts, wondering about moral issues, awed by the responsibilities of being a teacher, an experience seldom encountered so directly in the classroom. Yet if we look again at the conversation it seems innocuous enough, concerning as it does the "goodness" and "badness" of trees. Once again we have the impression that many levels of meaning are here involved. The teacher has become caught up with one of them, but it is only one of many. The conversation is rich with possibilities. It belongs truly within the habitat being presently explored.

The magical moment has come. Possessed with a wealth of alternatives, how shall selection among them be determined? Who now takes the initiative in conversation? There has been a pause. We have come to know something of the teacher's thoughts. We may assume that each child, occupied with his own thoughts, has followed a different and unique direction. The direction to be followed by the group may well depend upon who first breaks the silence. The teacher is unwilling to express her argument and continues her thinking. It is she who is in the process of learning. The teacher is not concerned to teach about the growth of trees, of which she knows nothing, nor momentarily is that a problem. She is not about to look up in secondary sources the facts of the matter. She is concerned with learning, her own learning. At the same time, the children are concerned with theirs. They are not attempting to learn from the teacher, nor even with the teacher, nor even from one another. Each child independently is thinking his own thoughts, exploring a personal direction, within the social sympathy of the group.

But what about the work task, the real reason for coming to look at trees? The teacher, still struggling with conventional reactions, sees this as the new curriculum. In a sense it is, except that the task may be the means of learning something other than itself. It may also be a place for retreat when what is the other learning becomes too difficult or too remote or for some other reason beyond the range of possibilities for the learner. It is not something that absolutely has to be done. Nor is it a framework. It is a beginning. It may be returned to at any time. It is common ground, common knowledge, and therefore a meeting place, when meetings become necessary. It provides stability when the learning gets tough.

In the episode of the tree, the learning for the teacher is tough, and she may well recall the work task. But for the moment the silence continues, and for the children this may be the most productive activity in the learning experience so far. But we could not know this by testing.

Let us observe what now happens:

PETER: We could still measure it.

TEACHER: What?

PETER: The tree. We want a tape.

MARY: All the trees. We'll have to measure them all.

FIONA: That'll take forever.

MARY: No it won't. I'll do those, and. . . .

TEACHER: Yes. I'm not clear what we want to measure yet. Peter said earlier something about measuring around the trunks.

PETER: Yep.

TEACHER: How would that help? (*Pause*) Look, what we really want to know is something about how trees grow. Right? Well, they grow out, and they grow up, and I suppose they also grow down. The roots, I mean.

PETER: We can't measure them.

TEACHER: Well, no. But there must be something we could do. Suppose we thought about something smaller than trees, or even a very small tree.

MARY: Could we grow our own tree?

FIONA: How could we do that?

MARY: Well, . . .

TEACHER: That's not a bad idea.

PETER: Hey! I know what we could do. There's a place where we bought our Christmas tree. It's quite a long way, but the man cuts them from the woods. He has them all sizes. He grows new ones, and. . . .

FIONA: He plants them?

PETER: Yes, and you can choose a size.

The teacher feels as excited as Peter, and yet she is also diffident. This is all going too far, too fast. Can they really take that kind of a trip, just the four of them, just to find out something—she is not at all sure what—about trees? The whole thing is quite ridiculous. There must be a book in the library that could answer the whole thing very simply. And yet. . . . That's the trouble. It would be too simple. The teacher knows that Peter would not be satisfied with that kind of explanation, that Fiona would probably not understand a word of it, that Mary would accept it, yet perhaps feel at the same time that something in the explanation was missing, that her questions were not truly answered. More than this, though, the teacher knows that they would all feel cheated. They want to know first hand. They want to solve the problem their own way. They need to know that they can solve the problem. This is what they need to learn. The trees are a secondary issue, incidental, second-order learning. Going off to see the trees isn't just a romantic bit of nonsense about the beauty of learning from nature. These children are for real. They want answers for real. It is the books that make romantic nonsense even in the name of science.

We might pause here to reflect that second-order learning, if translated to the conventional class, would be the substance of the curriculum. It would not be considered incidental. The realities of school reverse the realities of learning out of school. If the priorities are different, it is hard to see how school can be the preparation it so often claims to be.

In the school we have witnessed the explosion of learning. Now out of school we are seeing the same thing, with this difference, that the physical boundaries are not walls, and so the campus spreads beyond the confines of the school and of its vicinity. The physical learning area is much enlarged, and with it the range and diversity of possibilities. The episode of the tree exhibits physical range, but it is not yet over, and we need to continue our observations to see what diversity of learning occurs.

Contact is made with the tree man, and a half-day visit arranged. There are, however, domestic complications. It is very well for an individual teacher to go off for a half an hour with a few children, leaving two colleagues with a larger number of students, but to go off for a half a day creates undue strain. It is true that children help each other, but there is need for adult help, even if only to provide materials, to keep up the pace of work, to referee disputes, to support children when their own attempts fall short, simply to be there as a friend in need. This pressure could be relieved if more children were taken on the trip. The disadvantages of this are fairly obvious. The small group loses its sense of identity, and thus its purpose, so that the visit becomes an experience very different from the one designed by the children themselves. The tree man will obviously react very differently to a large number than to three students only. He might well be flattered by individual interest, but overwhelmed, if not angry, at a horde. The additional children have not participated in the learning process leading up to the visit, so that their interests in the proceedings would be very different from those of the learning group. Administratively, it makes a lot of sense to distribute the load more evenly, but from the learning point of view such a distribution would frustrate learning for those for and by whom the visit was especially planned. Our criterion is to maximize learning. Anything that gets in the way of learning is to be avoided.

Some teachers will argue the unfairness of such a decision. They may argue that it is unfair to leave the other two teachers to deal with such large numbers, and they may argue, too, that many children are being denied the opportunity of a visit. To them the matter is clear-cut. It can be measured. This is the most obvious criterion for fairness in the conventional school order, even though much is said concerning the fulfillment of the needs of children and of teachers. Somehow this criterion suggests that everyone's needs are alike.

We have all known the attempts of teachers to teach fairness to children. One particular example comes to mind. A young teacher, concerned that a seven-year-old boy did not understand the concept of fairness, took him aside to teach him.

TEACHER: You have two cookies. Here they are. Your friend Michael has none. That's not fair. What are you going to do about it?

GORDON: Oh, I'd give them to him.

TEACHER: How many would you give him?

GORDON: Both of them. I had my breakfast. He's always hungry.

TEACHER: But if you shared them, how many would you give him?

GORDON: Both of them, of course. He's hungry.

TEACHER: Suppose it wasn't cookies, but something else, like two balls. How would you share them?

GORDON: I'd give Michael one. He doesn't have many things, you know. And I'd give one to Pete. He can do all sorts of things with a ball. He. . . .

The teacher complained that she simply couldn't get across to Gordon the concept of fairness. From this isolated story it is hard indeed to know whether or not Gordon knew what the teacher thought he should, but in one sense he obviously knew a lot more! His concept of fairness equates with giving according to need. He knew about individual differences and preferences, and his criteria of fairness are much more sophisticated than simple division.

Some teachers will nevertheless sympathize with the teacher in this story. Perhaps she was insensitive to Gordon's generous nature, but she is a concerned teacher, trying to do her job, to teach. By now, though, we easily recognize why her attempts are so frustrating. She has an aim in mind, her aim, which she is trying to transfer to Gordon. We know, though, that the learner's aim is not the same as the teacher's. She is trying to teach her aim, which is, after all, a part of herself. She is trying to make Gordon in the likeness of herself. Be like me. Do like me. Know like me. Believe like me. This is what has to happen in the conventional system before the child learns. Children must accept the teacher's criteria. Gordon cannot learn what the teacher has to teach unless he subordinates himself to her, becomes like her. In the conventional system the morals that are learned are a part of that system. Now that we are operating in ways beyond the system, our values are changing, and thus also the criteria for fairness, or whatever virtue we choose.

The trouble is that in the conventional school system fairness is a dispensation from the hierarchy. In the new order fairness, like all else, is built in. It is part of the habitat, an integral part, not to be separated from the activities. Fairness cannot be distinguished as part of a curriculum, any more than punctuation or the sense of smell. The morals, the virtues, belong within the group, but not to a special part of it. Earlier the teacher struggled to bring a body of knowledge to the children. The struggle now is much the same—that is, if the teacher assumes that there are moral principles independent of society.

In the three lessons a city began to be built, and in the building of it students became citizens in it. The teacher too was a citizen, and at the same time she was also a student. As a student inhabiting the city, she could be a leading citizen, because she was a leading learner. Provided with this new kind of leadership, fairness becomes not something dispensed by the leader but a concept learned by and with the leader.

In the conventional system the school, the building, the curriculum, the social hierarchy, the roles, and the morals are all fixtures independent of the presence of children and students. It is a closed system, one that is concluded before education begins. In the new order nothing is independent. There are strong structural ties which harmonize what are usually thought of as distinctive entities, that is, teacher and student, content and method, practice and theory, morals and the intellect, society and the individual. We have seen this new way opening out of the old, by changing the old. The new system is not a closed system. It is public. It is open, infinitely capable of change. And it must continually change. Change is the index of learning. If nothing is learned, there will be no change and no need for change.

But what, many teachers will ask, does all this have to do with the one teacher who wants to take three children to see a man about some trees? Involved in this episode is a test of priorities. The learning of a few is at odds with the organization of the many. This is how a confrontation may grow. Confrontation, whatever else it may do, does not facilitate learning, and because of that it is to be avoided. The problem for the one teacher, then, becomes not simply how to make the arrangement for this one visit but how to establish, in general, a way of dealing with minority interests.

We are faced with a familiar problem, and one which in another context we have already solved. In the conventional class, preoccupied with curriculum requirements and the like, there is little room to schedule time for individual interests, either those of teachers or those of students. In the open class teachers and students alike share responsibilities in scheduling. Teachers pursue their interests, children theirs. There is individualized teaching and individualized learning. Our problem comes about only because we have extended spatial boundaries, not because we are unable to accept and respond to minority interests. Our problem, therefore, is not wholly new. It is clear that if we wish to extend our activities spatially, then that space must have in it the resources to fulfill our needs. Instead of thinking that such extension stretches our present resources beyond their limits, we should seek in that extension the additions to our resources. Education is not uni-dimensional. It is not just we who are opening out, but when we do, there are consequences and responses. If learning belongs not just in the school, then it is not just the school which is responsible for it. If learning belongs in society, it becomes the responsibility of society. When society learns this, society changes its behavior, changes itself.

It is true that society designates a place for learning, a school, and donates money for that school. Effectively, what happens is that the responsibility for education is given over to a professional body. Having done this, society then disclaims responsibility. Society pays money, the medium of exchange, thereby avoiding all contact with education. Money, however much, cannot buy learning, any more than it can buy love or peace. It does buy help. And schools can help, but ultimately the responsibility for education is in all of society. And responsibility means personal commitment. Many people are disenchanted by the results of professional educators and are unwilling to commit more money. But there are other things to give—time, materials, expertise. That is, after all, what the tree man will give.

So far in our opening up we have seen that the job of the teacher has been to bring together resources for a work task and then to lead learning in the task. In this new opening the job of the teacher is the same. The task is to visit the tree man. The preparation is in bringing together resources which will make that possible.

The teacher, then, will put the problem to her colleagues. She is very clear about what she wants to do, and she is equally clear that in the near future, in the next few weeks, the other teachers will find themselves in similar positions. Neighborhood excursions, the ten-minute walk, the half-hour interview, these sorts of things are no problem. It is the extended time periods—those of a half a day or more—which will put strain on teachers and on children that need special preparation. The extended periods will probably often involve a lapse of a few days between the initial need and the completion of arrangements. This being the case, one possibility is to write into the weekly program a time period of, for example, a half a day when some communal activity can be scheduled, that is, a large-group activity. Any lengthy visits by very small groups can be arranged to take place at the same time. The times do not need to be equal in length, but the communal activity, whether it is watching a film, attending a fire department demonstration, having a song session, or listening to a concert, should be such that the responsibility of performance is not wholly the teachers'. It is a way of bringing the community outside school into contact with the community in school. The sitting session might well be followed by a lengthy recess or outdoor recreation period. This in turn could be followed by another recognized quiet period, for library work or storytelling. Whatever the program arrangements for this time slot are, it is clear that they are different in kind from the rest of the week's activities. They are essentially designed for the large group, and their success depends upon the community spirit of the group.

There are other possibilities. The loss of one teacher for a half a day may be made up by assistance from student teachers, interested parents, or university or college people interested in the work of the group. Assistance of this kind will depend very largely upon the publicity campaign. If the activities are well known in the local community and by local colleges, then additional help of all kinds at all times may become readily available.

This participation may bring up a new problem for the regular teachers. Clearly, such help can contribute much, provided the helpers know they are expected to participate in activities, not to oversee activities. But at the same time, the teachers may well begin to wonder about their role as professionals. This applies both to the teachers who stay in the classrooms and to the teacher who visits the tree man. Their status is based upon specific training and statements of qualification. Their present work bears no relation to their previous training, and it becomes increasingly clear that parents, community people, and students can work alongside children in such a way that children come to learn to read, write, and count, practice all the basic skills, and learn about trees and much more even though these people have not been trained as teachers. This is, to put it mildly, disconcerting. But yet it is not unexpected, for it was only when the teacher herself became a student in her own classroom that she began to engender among the children the kinds of success in learning it seemed not possible to promote using the regular methods.

Thus the teacher may well begin to suspect that anyone can teach, trained or not. In one sense this is true: we are all teachers, just as we are all learners. How, then, can we justify the continuance of a professional group of teachers? If, as seems to be happening, education is returning to the community and the community is becoming involved in education, is there now a need for highly trained, specialized teachers? People with great skills, be they musicians, pastry cooks, or growers of trees, teach their skills to apprentices. These people are teachers of music, of pastry-making, and of tree-growing. What, then, is a teacher a teacher of? When we had a curriculum it was possible to say that the art teacher taught art or that the reading teacher taught reading, though in fact few children became artists, and remarkably few became skilled in reading. Now that we have abandoned the curriculum, even though children are becoming artists and readers, we can scarcely claim that we are teaching them how to do these things.

Suppose, then, we look not at the aim of teaching, which is, after all, what in the old convention we should have done, but at the new task of the teacher, the work that she is involved in, both in the class and on the visit. The teacher is all the time trying to maximize learning, the children's and her own. The teacher does not know about trees. Neither do the children. Their task is jointly to learn the task they have set themselves. And this will always be their task, over and over again. The more the teacher learns, the more the children will learn. The more they learn, the more they will be able to go on learning. The teacher, then, has to be the ablest learner. This is the teacher's special skill. The professional teacher has to be the kind of person who is able to learn supremely well, not one who has learned supremely well, not one who has achieved knowledge of this or that, but one who all the time is seen in the art of learning. A teacher is not one who knows, but one who knows how to come to knowledge.

By now the teachers of the group have learned the new organization by which they can make possible the extended units of small groups. Let us return to the episode of the tree.

A few days elapse before the visit, and each day the group goes out for a short while to look at trees. Peter measures around tree trunks. Mary makes a map to locate the trees they measure. These are numbered, and Fiona draws up a chart of each numbered tree for Peter to record his measurements. Together they try to work out what their measuring means. They search for a pattern. There are no leaves yet, but Peter notices differences in the bark and wants these put on the chart. That's a problem until a symbol is created for each kind of bark. This necessitates an identification key. First the children try words, but eventually they make a large key with bark rubbings. The teacher becomes aware that the children are in the process of creating a new language, and in a curious way she becomes aware herself of language as a set of symbols. She wants to tell children her understanding. She wants to tell them what they are doing. She wants to tell them about themselves. We have seen this situation before, after the first lesson, when suddenly the teacher understood that bridges span time and space. This need is her need and may be an intrusion, perhaps even a confusion, in the learning of the students. But the teacher has friends to share her needs, her discoveries, and her experiences with. Where once the teacher would have asked, "What more can I do?" she is now so involved in the doing that it is the choice between actions that needs discussion.

The group visits the tree man. He takes them to see parts of the plantation and shows them how to recognize the age of trees. He talks about seedlings and mature growths and about how to keep the trees healthy.

MARY: I still don't understand what makes a tree grow.

TREE MAN: It's hard to explain.

TEACHER: Suppose we take this branch. No, just this bit here, this bump. In two years from now will it be bigger? And will it still be in the same place or further out from the tree?

PETER: Of course it'll be bigger. Like knees.

TREE MAN: That's a good one.

MARY: I still don't see what makes it get bigger. I mean, I don't know how I get bigger.

TEACHER: And you see you everyday.

TREE MAN: Well, it's like this. All living things are made up of cells, little tiny units, and these divide and become more, and when there are more, then the whole thing gets bigger.

MARY: How do these things . . .

TREE MAN: Cells?

MARY: Cells. How do they divide. What makes them do that? Do they grow?

TREE MAN: Yes. No. Do you know, I don't really know the answer. You can see them under a microscope moving around, and the bit in the middle, the nucleus, pulls apart, and you get another cell, like this. (*He demonstrates, drawing on the ground with a stick.*)

MARY: But they move around. Then growing is a sort of moving?

The tree man looks very puzzled, and the teacher explains how originally they were talking about symmetry and how this seemed to affect the direction of movement in living things.

TREE MAN: Oh, well, trees do move. At least, they respond to light. You can see this very well with house plants.

He explains how the children might go away and do some experiments on their own to show how plants move. Then he takes them to a part of the plantation where there are some odd-shaped trees and explains how wind and weather affect growth in some directions more than others.

MARY: Then growing is a kind of movement.

TREE MAN: Well, I really never thought about it before, but yes, I suppose it is. I'll have to think about it some more.

FIONA: Can we have a look at those things under a microscope?

TREE MAN: Cells? I don't have the right equipment, but I'm sure they do at the university. They might help you out.

PETER: Let's go there.

TEACHER: I'll try to arrange it.

MARY: What really makes things grow?

TREE MAN: That's a good question.

MARY: You don't know?

TREE MAN: No. Not really.

FIONA: I know. God. That's what the minister said.

TREE MAN: Maybe.

Once again the teacher feels on the edge of a precipice. Open education is all very fine, but you can't control people. That is perhaps its chief virtue. People have to control themselves.

In the conventional system control comes before learning. Unless the teacher can control the class, make the class conform to an image, then the teacher cannot teach and the student cannot learn. The student has to surrender himself to the teacher in exchange for knowledge from and of the teacher.

If the new system is truly open, then the control is not separate from learning. If something is learned, then control also is learned—control of self, of thoughts, of actions, of skills, of human performance.

In the last piece of conversation with the tree man the teacher has no control over what is taught nor over what is learned. It is, in fact, very hard to say who has taught and who has learned. The episode of the tree ends in a mystery. The man who knows about trees does not know about trees. He does not know about God. This is the reality of the world we live in. This is the reality that children have to know.

In a book things are different. The cell formations are set out, explained, named, and the process is described. If there is doubt, this doubt is stated. Doubt, in a book, is a positive statement. But in the conversation doubt is doubt, not positive, not negative, but just doubt. It has depth. It is not a plain statement on a flat page.

The literary tradition of learning, which in past decades has been of untold value in disseminating the accumulated knowledge of the ages, threatens now to stifle learning. In education books have become, like money, mediums of exchange, by which contact with what is written about may be wholly avoided and yet claimed to be known. It is not that books are not useful still, but that they belong to the closed system. We have seen how in the open class resources, including the teacher, come to be used very differently than in the conventional class. Our tree group may now return to the school to books, but they will read them in a wholly new way. Books too can become open.

The mystery continues. Some time later the tree man calls the school. He has found out where the children can go to do some microscope work in a properly equipped laboratory. Our story, after all, has not ended.

CHAPTER ELEVEN

Seminar

ELLEN: When I agreed to open this meeting I had not anticipated my task would be difficult. I must confess, I've always rather enjoyed this sort of thing. It's usually not too hard to ask some kind of general question that gets everyone going. But this time, though I found a whole lot of questions I wanted to ask, I really didn't think it appropriate to ask them. The book comes out so strongly against the asking of questions! And then I began thinking what else I might do, rather like the narrators in the book. The trouble was that there are so many things I want to say, yet they are all rather personal. In the end it seemed to me that it really didn't much matter where I began, so long as I began, again an echo of what seems to be a principle of open education. So here I am, beginning.

ROBERT: O.K. so you've begun. But where does that leave us? Asking an opening question? I really can't see why questions are so bad. And they are used in the book, like the theme question.

SARAH: What more can I do?

ROBERT: Yes.

SARAH: But surely that question is asked by a teacher, by a lot of teachers. I mean, it's a sort of quote.

ROBERT: Well, yes. But why can't a starting point begin with a question? Surely that's what a starting point is.

SARAH: If you mean it sets you off on a quest, perhaps. But what makes you ask the question? Isn't there something that precedes it?

MIKE: Sure there is. How can you ask about something you don't know?

ROBERT: Very easily. I don't know what it's like to walk on the moon, but I can ask what it's like.

MIKE: But you can't ask the question unless you know that there is a moon to be walked on. So you do know something before you ask the question.

TOM: Look, all this is pretty philosophical sort of stuff, and I'd rather talk about the more practical side. It seems to me that the book is full of practical suggestions, but I don't think they're practical for me.

ELLEN: Can you explain a bit?

TOM: Well, take, for instance, the very first lesson, the building of the bridge. The instructions are perfectly clear, and I can really see it happening, but not in my class. I mean, the kids would just be all over the room if I didn't jump on them all the time.

MIKE: If you didn't jump on them all the time they might feel differently.

TOM: Oh, come on, man, you know better than that. This whole thing sounds just great, but I'd like to meet the guy who could make it work.

ELLEN: Why are you so sure that that man isn't you?

TOM: Look, you've got to be kidding. You should just see my class. They're just spoiling for a fight, with me, with anyone. Give them half a chance and they'd break each others' necks.

MIKE: You gave as your example lesson one, the building of a bridge. In the book that is a metaphor for getting through to kids and having them get through to you. You've got a problem, though. I don't know your class, and the problem isn't like the one in the book. Sounds to me as though the kids need to build a bridge between themselves, to get through to one another.

ROBERT: Oh, great.

MIKE: Well?

TOM: Well, I don't know.

ROBERT: Look, let's face it. Where's the message? You're talking about getting through to kids. I don't get it. The book doesn't get through to me. What chapter really fulfills its title, for example, and if that isn't confusion enough, you can take any bit out of a chapter and find that it has a whole lot of different meanings. The whole thing is just so misleading.

MIKE: Oh, come on. It has a very simple form. It goes on from A to B. It's a logical progression. The classroom as it is, then what it might become, and, finally, what a school might become.

ROBERT: Sure, that's logical. But it's so absurd and contrived. In the first place, we don't know whether this is fact or fiction. The children are named, but is it a real class? How big is it? And another thing, no statement is ever made about what grade it is.

MIKE: I take it you're talking about the three-lesson class.

ROBERT: Yes.

MIKE: Hm, you're right there. I never noticed that. I sort of assumed it was my own.

ELLEN: I said at the beginning that I had a lot of personal questions, and most of them came out of that class, so to speak. I wanted to ask many times how old is so and so.

SARAH: My experience is similar. I mean, I kind of identified with the teacher of the class. But now it occurs to me that I couldn't have done this if I'd been told it was grade five, for example. I teach grade three.

ELLEN: I teach grade five.

MIKE: Well, there you are, then. There's the reason.

ROBERT: O.K., but that makes the whole thing fiction.

ELLEN: Well, so what? I mean, that doesn't seem such a bad thing.

ROBERT: No? How can you believe in the progression if it didn't really happen? It's all just a game.

ELLEN: No. I don't think you can say that.

ROBERT: I just did.

ELLEN: Well, all right, you can say it. But I think you can say other things, too. For example, . . .

SARAH: I've got it. Excuse me.

ELLEN: It's O.K. Go ahead.

SARAH: Robert said it's just a game. Right? Well, all through the book everytime something new has to be learned by the teacher the narrators say "play." Now if the book is "just a game," as you say, and if you treat it that way—play with it, so to speak—then you might learn from it. The book is a sort of metaphor.

TOM: That makes it kind of complicated.

ELLEN: How do you mean?

TOM: Well, as Robert said, you take a thing in the book and it always turns out to mean something else. And now here we are taking the whole book and doing just that. I really need that starting point because I'm going around in circles.

ELLEN: That would be like exploring a habitat.

ROBERT: Oh, shut up.

ELLEN: No, but it would.

ROBERT: If you say so.

ELLEN: Look, you really don't think too much of this book, do you? Yet I suspect some of us here have found it useful, and it seems to me that we ought at least to explore what we do think is useful.

SARAH: I'd like to say something about what I found useful. In a way, it's rather personal but—well, here goes. In Chapter Seven, I think it is, and some other places, too, but especially there, there's a tremendous emphasis on feelings, where beginning a new habitat is described. This recognition that teachers do have feelings came as real relief. I feel I don't need to pretend quite so much. I always felt I ought to be more intelligent and that I ought to know a lot more. Well, now I feel as though I really am allowed to feel sad in the classroom. I've got a right to feel depressed. The book's not going to jump down my throat and tell me what a bad teacher I am.

MIKE: It's interesting that you should talk about feelings. I often got the impression that the book was written about me. It was sometimes uncanny. Your talking about Chapter Seven still reminds me. I was really had. I kept thinking to myself it's obvious how you use the events of the afternoon group in the reading program. I really went along with that first idea. I imagined myself setting up reading groups around the centers of interest—shades of college teaching—and everything seemed to fall into place. And then it fell out of place. And so did I. Why couldn't I do what seemed obvious and reasonable? And then when I got to the end of that chapter I was excited, and kind of dazed, too. This totality that kept getting talked about really was a totality, not a thing in a classroom anymore. I just felt overwhelmed by its enormity. I couldn't ever have got there by myself, logically, I mean.

SARAH: You know, I think the book kept doing that, leading you along a path, the one that seemed obvious, and then somehow entering a whole new perspective. I don't really know what to call it.

MIKE: Totality?

SARAH: Well, yes, I suppose so. Only I don't much like the word.

ELLEN: Well, all right. But it seems to fit the experience we had when we were reading.

SARAH: Um.

ROBERT: Wouldn't it have been better if that first part of Chapter Seven had been cut out? I mean, it's just a waste of time taking everybody along the wrong path like that.

MIKE: No, I don't think so. In a way, I think that's the whole point. You see, I thought I understood, and I wouldn't have found out that I didn't if I hadn't gone along what seemed to be my line of thinking.

ELLEN: Isn't that why a lot of teachers, if you ask them what they're doing, always think they're really with it, because they have interest groups and all that sort of thing? It kind of looks the same from the outside, and everyone is fooled.

ROBERT: But surely it is the same. In my classes we've been doing these sorts of things for years, playing games with words. The kids love it. They write lots of good stuff. The principal goes along with it. I really can't see . . .

MIKE: That's it. You've said it. That's really it. You've been doing it for years. But it hasn't changed you. You haven't learned. Don't you see?

ROBERT: No, I don't.

MIKE: Look, you haven't learned in your class. And you haven't learned from the book, either. I mean, what do you make of that?

ROBERT: What should I make of it?

ELLEN: Somewhere in the book there's a bit about confrontation, and how this is not a learning situation. It seems to me that we ought to challenge the book rather than one another.

TOM: I thought I'd done that. As I said, it's great. But how do you make it work?

ROBERT: I just can't go along with that. The book is full of weakness. It's also very misleading. It starts with the supposition of a teacher in a classroom trying to do a little better and ends with a new world order.

SARAH: Yes, but you don't have to go all the way. You can start where you are and just keep on trying.

MIKE: Keep on learning.

SARAH: Yes.

ROBERT: Look, the book is quite specific. Once you've started, you just can't stop or you're done for. If you ever did get started, you'd ruin your career.

SARAH: If you stopped, perhaps. But then I think you'd ruin it even if you never started, because it's just obvious that things aren't working now and if we don't get started soon we've had it.

ROBERT: O.K. So what makes you so sure you're going to get started in the right direction? The book does assume a direction. That's another part of its false logic.

MIKE: You really don't like the book, do you?

ROBERT: No. I just think it's a lot of nonsense, no better and no worse than a lot of other stuff.

SARAH: You've got to admit it's different, though.

ROBERT: All right. But it still doesn't help.

ELLEN: What would help you?

ROBERT: I don't know. It just seems as though everyone's trying to make an issue out of schools. If everyone keeps saying there is something wrong with them, then people get to believing it.

ELLEN: Do you believe it?

ROBERT: I don't know.

ELLEN: But you do know.

ROBERT: No, I really don't.

ELLEN: Why are you here?

ROBERT: I can't answer.

TOM: I just thought of something. This thing about schools all being wrong, I'm not sure the book really says that. I certainly got that impression, but now that I think about it, I don't know that a judgment is ever really passed.

MIKE: What about that bit right at the beginning where a regular-type situation . . .

TOM: Yes, but somehow that's not really saying things are wrong, only that if you do A, then B follows.

SARAH: That's right. And if you don't want B, then you'd better do something else.

TOM: Yes.

MIKE: I still think I'd put it more strongly, because it does seem to me that the impression created by the book, whether it says so or not, and I'd like to check on that, is that the present situation is all wrong. The whole point is that its suggestions for a new line of thinking are right, or at least better. Isn't that so?

SARAH: Couldn't we put it in terms of use? I mean, the old system, the conventions, aren't useful any more, and we need a new use.

TOM: That's O.K. with me, though I don't think the book puts it that way.

ELLEN: It's a useful thought, though.

ROBERT: If I remember right, somewhere, maybe in several places, great importance is attached to not making judgments, and yet there's a part in Chapter Seven where the kids are playing with words, and one of them is especially funny, and the teacher says, "You're absolutely right, Jimmy." Well, that's judgment. And praise too, incidentally. And that's something else. Why not praise kids for goood work?

SARAH: You know, I don't think that was said as a judgment, or as praise. It seems to me the teacher was having a good time, and a good laugh. It's just a friendly response.

TOM: It's not that kind of judgment that worries me. The trouble is that there are tests and things, and I've just got to face these. I know that there's that bit about spellings or spelling tests or something, and the kids being able to do it a lot better, but that's not the only kind of test they take. And what about records? It's all these practical, everyday things that bug me. How do I cope with this?

SARAH: I kind of sympathize with you there. I found a real problem when I first read the book. I couldn't find what I wanted without reading the whole thing. Like you, I was interested in what kinds of records a teacher would keep in the new scheme. And what about testing and that kind of thing? But there isn't an index, and I had to research the book to find what I wanted.

ELLEN: Yes, I know just what you mean. But in a funny way I suspect that is part of the new scheme. Things are not broken down into testing, records, retesting, and so on. This is all part of the totality the book insists on. And you can't index a totality.

TOM: But surely some things are more important than others, and it would be good to have a few headings.

ELLEN: Perhaps. But then, what you think is important is not what I think is important, nor what Robert or Sarah or Mike thinks is important. This shows up in what we've been talking about just now. The whole book is really like the lesson, or the three lessons. I mean, it's a sort of metaphor, or a reflection. Something like that. It leaves us to choose what we think is important. It doesn't do the judging for us.

TOM: That's a great thought. But I still think there are some things everyone would agree on as being more important, and that you can't approach everything as a totality. There just isn't time. In the interest of efficiency you just have to accept some things.

ROBERT: Now you're really saying something. A good teacher chooses what's best for the kids.

MIKE: No, no, no! If you do the choosing, they can never know it is the best, only that you think it is. Don't you see that? You stop their learning. That's what's so good about the book. It's about learning. It doesn't matter whether the teacher is making a right choice or a best choice, the fact is that the learner has to make the choice. If it's a wrong choice, there is one set of consequences. If it's a right choice, there is another. The learners can judge from the consequences. Don't you see? They choose and they judge.

ROBERT: Look, if what you're saying is true, and I don't think it is— but let's suppose it is—why in heaven's name does anyone need a teacher?

SARAH: To provide the choices. That's the habitat as I see it. It has in it all sorts of alternatives.

ROBERT: O.K. But lots of times I provide choices in my class. Kids like to choose what they can do sometimes.

MIKE: Only sometimes?

ELLEN: Could you perhaps give us an example?

ROBERT: All right We've been doing a project on Indians. We have five groups set up. One is working on making a model of an Indian village. Another group is making tools, another costumes, and another scenery. We plan to have a little play. And the other group is doing some research on the history of some of the chief tribes.

ELLEN: The children can choose whichever group they want to work in?

ROBERT: Certainly.

MIKE: Did they also choose the groups?

ROBERT: How do you mean?

MIKE: Well, how did the five groups come into being?

ROBERT: Oh, I see. Well, we just decided what sorts of things we wanted to do, and there seemed to be five things, so we made five groups.

MIKE: I'm still not clear. You say "we." How did the subject of Indians come up?

ROBERT: It didn't. It's there. It's a regular part of the curriculum.

MIKE: In other words, the kids didn't really choose.

ROBERT: They certainly did. They could work in any of the groups. And if they wanted to form another group, they could do that, too.

ELLEN: In other words, you did make choices available.

ROBERT: Yes.

SARAH: I understand that, but somehow the ultimate choice isn't there. Isn't that what you meant, Mike? I mean, it had to be Indians. And you had to approve the choices. The children were really choosing your choices.

ROBERT: No. I don't agree. As I said, they could choose to have another group if they wanted.

SARAH: But it would have to be about Indians.

ROBERT: Yes, I don't see that that is a problem. If you like, I provided an Indian habitat.

MIKE: Oh, no!

ELLEN: I'm not sure that I can make the distinction between what you do and what gets done in the book, but I do feel that they are different.

SARAH: The way the groups begin is different, isn't it? That first lesson, the bridge-building lesson, that didn't have any groups. I'm just trying to think. After that the teacher grouped the bridges together. Then in the next lesson the kids worked in the groups she had made. Yes, I guess it is the same, after all.

MIKE: No, it may look the same, but it isn't. For a start the kids could always change groups, from smaller ones or different ones or what they wanted. Second, the groups determined what they were going to do. They didn't decide beforehand, "We are going to make costumes" or whatever it was. The group and its task grew together, and as it went along it changed. Surely the whole distinction is that yours is made more or less fixed. Everyone knows what the groups are and what they're for, why they are. But in the book no one knows. They know what they are doing, but they're not fixed.

SARAH: They're open.

MIKE: Precisely!

ROBERT: Look, that's not altogether true. Take the Silly Season business. The whole point of that was the performance.

MIKE: Was it? I thought it was publicity.

ROBERT: Well, all right, publicity. But the kids worked toward the performance. That was an end.

MIKE: Except that it wasn't. It was the beginning of getting to work outside the classroom and outside of class. I mean, you could say that when a bridge is built, the bridge is the end. Or that when the race track is complete that is the end. But the fact is that there is no end, or if there is, it turns out to be the beginning of something. Incidentally, I liked that bit about the exit being an entrance—you know, in the last chapter when they get out of school. There's just something very positive about it all. You just have to keep on going.

SARAH: I felt like I kept on beginning again.

TOM: Well, I don't know. I've been listening, but I'm really confused. I feel I'd like to begin, but I still can't see this doing anything for me. We sort of go back and forth between the philosophical stuff and the practical, as if we don't know where we are.

SARAH: I think we do know where we are. We're in the middle of things, in a habitat. We can go back and forth, because somehow we must.

ELLEN: It seems to me we're acting out the book. We've got two sides here. Robert seems happy with the way things are. Right?

ROBERT: I think they could be better.

ELLEN: Well, sure, but by and large you'd stake your claim with what you've got.

ROBERT: Yes.

ELLEN: And then there's Mike and maybe you, Sarah. That's the other extreme. I'm going to leave you and me out of it for the moment, Tom. The point is that the two sides are represented, and yet it seems to me we are finding out a lot about the book. This must be, well—I don't really know now what I wanted to say. It got away from me.

SARAH: I think I kind of have an idea about it. The trouble is, I'm not sure about the words. It seems to me we're being both practical and theoretical at the same time.

ELLEN: Integrated?

SARAH: Yes, integrated! About a book which is integrated. I mean, it really is. That's what's really confusing us. In a way, it's easier to see in the book. You know, in the middle of one teaching point something quite different seems to come in, like with fairness in the middle of the tree episode. It doesn't really belong, and yet what would happen without it?

ROBERT: It would just get put in some other place.

ELLEN: No, I don't think so. You see, I keep coming back to the logic of the whole thing. I can see that. It's my starting point. Then I can't help thinking that all the bits must somehow be logical too.

SARAH: You know, it's good you should say that, I mean about the whole book being your starting point. Isn't that what the book says somewhere? Something like it anyhow. I think it was in the bit about learning to read. Somehow you have to take the whole of language, not just twenty spellings.

ROBERT: I'd like to take this whole thing about logic. I agree you can make an argument for a logical progression if you look at the chapter headings. The only thing is that what goes in the chapters just doesn't, in my mind, have anything to do with the headings. Within the chapters there is all sorts of disorder and disorganization. We've talked a bit about this before. But there are just so many examples of it. There's that great explanation about lesson plans, and making them in retrospect. Then what happens? You destroy the lesson and all the plans along with it. That's just a waste of the reader's time.

TOM: I think there are examples of disorder, but I don't think that's one of them. I just don't agree that's a waste of time. If you didn't understand the retrospect bit first, how could you get an understanding that the new system really has a structure which replaces the old plan?

ROBERT: Well, all right. Maybe you've got a point there. But wouldn't you say that there's an awful lot of wasteful repetition? It all seems so unauthoritative. It's not a scholarly work, of course, but when you talk about logic, it seems to me the book really tries to appeal to feelings, not rationality.

SARAH: I was the one who kind of came out on the side of feelings, and maybe you're right about this, but does this matter? That early chapter, about classroom conversation and what you could learn from it really stayed with me through the book. I felt all the time that the book was talking to me. I couldn't talk back, but I kind of felt involved. It's not somehow a written book, although you say, or rather Ellen said, its chapters are logical. What happens in them is disorderly, like someone is really speaking and thinking and learning in a disordered fashion and yet coming always to a conclusion.

MIKE: A conclusion? Surely not. The thing is never concluded. There's always more.

SARAH: Well, yes, that's true. But you do get somewhere. I guess I'm talking about learning.

MIKE: That's the point. You do keep on going. It's a dynamic.

ELLEN: The thing that I chiefly suspect is that so often it makes sense! When I'm learning I never make sense. It's too plausible. There isn't a rationale for learning. It just happens. That's what I feel about my learning. And sometimes I got irritated at the presumption in the book that now I could understand this or that. Sometimes I felt it just took too much for granted.

ROBERT: Oh yes, I think it did. I think it takes an awful lot for granted. For a book that seems to side with freedom of the individual, all this stuff about individualized teaching and learning, it seemed to be remarkably dictatorial.

ELLEN: Could you explain a bit more?

ROBERT: The simplest example that comes to mind is the three lessons. How can a whole system be changed by just three lessons? Even if it were three years, it would be staggering. But three lessons! That is just utter stupidity. And yet you have to accept this if the book means anything at all. Then again it purports to answer a lot of problems, but just look at the problems it creates. That never gets a mention! Suppose you put three classes together. What about continuity? What happens next year? I think we mentioned grades before. But suppose they were all different grades together. And what about the parents? They'd have something to say. Over and over again the dictator is at work here. You complained when I said the teacher knows best what is good for kids, but what about the teacher in the book? She admits she doesn't know, and then she proposes all sorts of crazy innovations. There's not a shred of evidence that any of them will work.

TOM: Perhaps not. But then there's no evidence that they will not work.

ROBERT: But you said yourself you couldn't do it.

TOM: Yes, I did. And I still don't see how, but I still think there's a lot in it.

ELLEN: Would it help to say what you liked about it?

TOM: I find that hard. We've talked about logic and we've talked about feelings, but I don't think I see the book like that at all. I mean, it's really very practical. I get a picture of teachers doing things in the classroom and kids really having a great time. There are a lot of down to earth ideas. Like that one about the mobiles. Well, I just think that's great.

ROBERT: But how is that going to help you teach $2 + 2 = 4$?

MIKE: $2 + 2 = 4$. That is symmetry. That's what it's about.

ROBERT: You may see that. But what child is going to?

MIKE: Look, you can teach a parrot to say $2 + 2$, just as well as you can teach a child. But that isn't enough, and you know it. What the mobile does is explain what an equation is all about. It balances. You're teaching not just $2 + 2 = 4$, but $a + b = c$. The whole thing is much more sophisticated, but I bet any child, once he's built a mobile and got it balanced, knows a darn sight more about math than the parrot.

ROBERT: But you don't have any proof?

MIKE: Certainly I've got proof. I'm not a parrot.

SARAH: Surely proof isn't necessary, not for everything?

ROBERT: Look, I'm really concerned that you can accept what seems to me a fantastic hoax. Ours is a responsible job. We've got to be sure we're doing the right thing, or at least the best that we can do. And you all seem to be dead set on going off and trying out a lot of stuff that may be all right, and then again may not be. You can't know till you've tried. Suppose you do try it, and it's a disaster. What about the kids? They're going to suffer because of you.

ELLEN: They're probably going to suffer because of us all. We are all human. None of us is right. And I think we should remember that. What we've got to do is to find alternatives so that we can choose what we think is best. Then we can blame ourselves for making the wrong choice, and not somebody else. We've got to live with our own consequences. At the moment all we can do is live with the consequences of a system. One of the things that struck me in the second part of the book, where there were two schools, the regular one, and the open one, was that there was an alternative. I don't think enough was made of this in the book. If Robert feels very strongly that things are O.K. the way they are, then that's fine. And if Mike wants them differently, then that's fine too.

SARAH: Don't you think that kids, or their parents, anyway, should do the choosing?

ELLEN: Yes, I do.

SARAH: That doesn't come over in the book.

ELLEN: No. And I think Robert had a good point when he said that some things were dictatorial.

SARAH: It seems as though we're back to order and disorder.

MIKE: I don't follow.

SARAH: Well, I'm not sure that I do, either. That makes disorder. Yet I have connections, and that makes me feel good, secure. That's a kind of order.

MIKE: Oh, I thought you were talking about the book.

TOM: But in a way you are still talking about the book, aren't you? You said yourself that's how the book is. I don't think we really finished with that argument. I'd like to go back and look at it again. It's funny. I like to know what I'm doing, but there's a puzzle here, and I want to sort it out a bit. You said, somebody said, there is a discrepancy between the chapter headings and what goes on in the chapters. And I agree. You could very well head them social studies, language arts, and math, for example. Then it would be a book about the curriculum, and yet it clearly isn't that. Do you see what my puzzle is?

MIKE: Yes, but I don't see why it can't be explained. Surely it's quite simple. You have to start somewhere, so you start with the curriculum and grow out of it.

TOM: I see that explanation. Yes, that fits. But I still don't see why the chapters are headed the way they are.

ROBERT: That's all part of the book.

SARAH: Don't the headings describe the result of what goes on? For example, "The Explosion of Learning." I got quite a shock at the end of that, because I'd forgotten what it was supposed to be about. Then it sort of exploded on me. And I hadn't realized that till now.

ELLEN: You know, I think this is more complex even than that. Usually chapter headings are about what goes on. They describe in some way the process. But these describe the end, and yet they come at the beginning, the beginning of the chapter. And this is very strange because there is a preoccupation throughout the book with not knowing the end. Do you see what I mean? Everything is sort of reversed.

SARAH: What we've been calling disorder is a different kind of order? I need to think about this.

MIKE: This is kind of exciting. I mean, it means more than it seems to mean.

ROBERT: I think we're making altogether too much of it. It's just another contrivance.

MIKE: Look, suppose it is just another contrivance, all part of that hoax you keep talking about. It just could be we might learn something anyway.

ROBERT: I doubt it.

MIKE: For heaven's sake, man, if you doubt, your kids are going to doubt. I'm glad I'm not in your class. You make me real angry.

SARAH: Hey, take it easy, will you. I want to think.

ELLEN: Do you mind if I go on thinking out loud? The headings seem to apply to the result of the chapter, the destruction of the lesson, and then the class, and so forth. The idea is, in the book, that you're always trying to learn something, but you don't know what it is. So you set off in one direction and when you've gone along the way you can look back and see what you've also learned, things you didn't expect. This is like the child's learning. The teachers can't really know what they have to learn, and neither can they, but give them half a chance to learn something and they may also learn something else. I think I see meaning there.

Yes, I don't think it is quite so odd as it seems. We are looking at the book in retrospect. The teacher looks at the lesson in retrospect. The chapter looks at the heading in retrospect. That's not the right order. But you see what I mean?

SARAH: It's reflective, reflective, reflective.

MIKE: Help!

SARAH: Yes, I think I see. It's the metaphor again.

TOM: You're going to have to explain.

SARAH: I'm not sure I can yet.

ROBERT: You're making a mystery out of the whole thing. You can hide anything behind a metaphor. It seems to me this is just another example of disorder. Here's a book about open education, yet it revels in mystery. Doesn't that sound pretty suspicious to you?

SARAH: When you put it like that I guess it does. But you've played around with meanings.

ROBERT: But the book does nothing else. It even encourages teachers to do just that. So I don't know why you're complaining about me.

ELLEN: Yes. But it also seeks a totality, and you are, I think, whether you know it or not, breaking down that totality so that it doesn't make sense.

ROBERT: Now, you're talking just like the book. The parts don't make sense, but the whole does. Isn't that what you're saying? If you take the curriculum or the administration or "any one thing," I think I'm quoting correctly, then it doesn't make sense? So you've got to take the whole. But does that make sense? If the parts don't make sense, I don't see how the whole can.

MIKE: You don't see, but somebody else might, and that somebody else might be a child.

ELLEN: Look, I think you can look at it this way. Each part alone can be made to make sense. I mean, you could have a good curriculum and a good administration. But if you then put those two together, they might very well conflict with one another. So really you have to start with the whole thing, the totality, so that the whole thing makes sense. Could you accept that?

ROBERT: Yeah. I could accept that, but for one thing, the whole has to be broken down into parts, and my understanding of that is the way things are now. There is the head administration, then this is broken down into local administration, and so on, all down the system.

SARAH: Isn't the point not so much about parts and wholes, but about relations, which I think means making things come to a whole. In this sense the whole is always growing. It's the habitat. It's not static, it's always being made. That was my impression.

TOM: It says somewhere something about the habitat growing with the people in it.

SARAH: Yes. I mean, that's different from starting at the top. The top isn't the whole at all.

TOM: If I understood correctly about the habitat business, there isn't a bottom, either. I get a kind of circular picture. I'm not sure about whether it has a center or not.

ROBERT: It's like this meeting. We just go around in circles.

TOM: No. I don't think that's fair.

ROBERT: You really think you've got something out of it?

TOM: Well, I haven't answered my problem yet, but, yes, I think I understand more now than I did when we started.

ROBERT: What, for instance?

TOM: It may sound silly to you, but I think I can wait to solve my problem. I came in and I really wanted an answer, and now I think I can wait for one.

ROBERT: And do you think you'll get an answer by waiting?

TOM: I don't know. I can't really explain, but I feel I need to wait a bit. Like I need to find out something else first.

ROBERT: Like what?

TOM: Look, don't keep bugging me, man. I don't know. I mean, if I did know, I wouldn't have to learn.

ROBERT: You sound as if you're quoting.

TOM: Well, I'm not.

SARAH: I think you'll find out.

TOM: Why?

SARAH: I don't know. But I just think you will.

ELLEN: In a certain sense all discussions like this go around in circles, so I don't think we can blame it on the book.

ROBERT: Look, I admit I've been pretty critical of this whole thing, partly because, as I said, it's misleading, and therefore potentially dangerous. And I really do have strong feelings about that. I just think we should be very careful about changing things which have grown up over the years. It would be a terrible thing to destroy what it has taken generations to build.

ELLEN: I think many people feel the same way. On the other hand, this is the age of change. It's not just education, but every aspect of society is in a state of flux. All the traditions are in question. Women want their rights. War is becoming unethical. Marriage is outmoded. It's not somehow that we are proposing to destroy a tradition. The fact is, the process is underway, and we have to live with it.

ROBERT: Granted, there are changes taking place in society, but isn't that a good reason for providing some stability? Surely we're not looking for chaos, and education should provide a refuge, something fixed and firm that everyone can hold to.

ELLEN: It's true, I think, that people do need a refuge—security if you like—but I don't think that this should necessarily be fixed, or even that it should be fixed at all, because if it is, it sooner or later becomes itself challenged. I don't see why stability has to be stable in the sense of fixed. Stability, too, can, I think, go along with change, or rather it has to do this.

ROBERT: I don't get that at all.

ELLEN: Think of it this way. We are going at great speed, accelerating all the time. We have a direction, a flight path, though our destination is unknown and unknowable. The best that we can do is keep our craft well trimmed, stable, so that it functions well in flight, so that we can deal with emergencies as they arise, so that we ourselves are not the emergency. This could be done. The stability goes along with the craft, both moving at great speed.

ROBERT: Yes, I see that. But I also see that though the stabilizing system is moving with respect to whatever is outside the craft, it is not moving with respect to the craft itself. As you say, it goes along with it. In your analogy it seems to me we are in the craft, or even that we are the craft. I'm not clear about this. But anyway, with respect to the craft, the stability system is stable, is still, which is how I think education should be. It is the one fixed point in the universe.

MIKE: If it is the one fixed point, it is also alien to the universe.

TOM: Look, this argument is ridiculous. The analogy won't work. I agree that education and change somehow go together. I also think that educators are out of step with education. They don't change so fast. That is why people learn more out of school than in. I don't really care much about the principles. I just think we ought to face the facts. And I think the book does that. It takes, in the beginning, anyway, real teachers, in real classrooms, with real problems. And it tries to do something about it. As I said, it's a practical book.

ROBERT: And do you think it's practical to get outside the school to answer the problems? That seems to be the answer.

SARAH: I've just had a very strange thought. Well, maybe it's not so strange. But when you said that just now, about how the book starts, with real teachers and stuff, I remember how that first problem was overcome, about the building of the bridge. The idea of crossing came because we went outside the school. I forget, exactly, but it was something like how would you really cross a bridge if you weren't a teacher and you weren't in school? And then you, Robert, asked, "Is it practical to get outside the school?" It's the same thing. At the beginning of the book you do it in your mind, and at the end of the book you do it for real. What I think I'm saying is that the book is the lesson and the learning. I'm not quite sure what I'm saying. Do you see what I mean?

ELLEN: I see something. In fact, I think I see a whole lot of things.

ROBERT: It looks to me like another device. It's all part of the structure of the book. It's like a plot.

SARAH: If it is part of the structure of the book, couldn't it also be part of the structure of learning? I begin to feel as though the book is learning, and I'm learning about the book.

MIKE: That makes the book your teacher, doesn't it?

ROBERT: You want to be careful about that. After all, the book doesn't favor book learning. Incidentally, that is another example of its ill-conceived logic.

MIKE: Maybe not, though. It looks as though we're verging on another mystery.

ROBERT: Motivation for the new lesson?

ELLEN: I feel a bit like Sarah felt earlier. I want some time to think.

TOM: Think aloud again. Can you? That was kind of helpful.

ELLEN: Thank you. I'll try. I'm not sure how to begin. There seems like a beginning going out and an ending going out. Perhaps there are other reflections like this. Is there something, for example, that corresponds with the three lessons, reflects them, so to speak?

SARAH: How about the three teachers?

ELLEN: Maybe, but they could have been any number.

MIKE: But there were three.

ELLEN: Yes. But I don't see any meaning there.

SARAH: No.

ELLEN: The three lessons were social studies. Is there something that corresponds to that? Yes, of course there is. Yes, I begin to get it. Look, the social studies in the three lessons is about building a model city and inhabiting it. The social studies at the end of the book is going out into the city to remodel it and reinhabit it. Isn't that it? I want to think some more.

TOM: We want a new word. I mean, it begins with social studies, and it ends with social something else.

SARAH: Social beings?

MIKE: Hey, that's great!

TOM: But it's more than that, isn't it? It's not just that the inhabitants, so to speak, have become socialized, but . . .

MIKE: But what?

TOM: I don't know. The studies part has been replaced by reality, right? But study is something you do in private, so what is it that has become public? Do you see what I mean? There's something missing.

SARAH: I'm not sure I understand.

TOM: Well, I don't either, but I've got the feeling I'm on to something. It's funny, I feel as though I've got a clue. The book talked about clues in the beginning. And I couldn't understand why things were called clues. Well, I think I understand that now, anyway. I'd like to go back and read that beginning bit. Maybe I'll get some more clues.

ELLEN: I wonder if we can work the other way on. I mean, suppose we looked at the end and then tried to find parallels with the beginning. Take, for example, the episode of the tree. That seemed a very strange story.

TOM: Why did you think it was strange?

ELLEN: Well, it seemed a very unlikely sort of thing to be studying in the middle of a city. In a way, I suppose the city was a very unlikely thing to be studying in the middle of a classroom. There seems to be some sort of tie in there, but I don't see what.

SARAH: Wasn't it rather an unlikely way to study a tree? I mean, it's movement. It's funny, I'm starting to look for unlikely things, clues maybe. If you're going to choose a living thing as opposite as possible to a city, a tree is a good example, isn't it? It just stands still.

MIKE: The tree is an individual and the city is a lot of individuals?

SARAH: That would make a progression from the social to the individual. That doesn't seem to make sense. Unless . . .

ELLEN: Go on.

SARAH: Unless it signifies somehow that when the individual is out there, in the city, in the society, he finds himself, and when

Seminar

he is in the classroom being told to sit still and be quiet and be by himself, he becomes part of—part of a gang? That doesn't seem quite right.

MIKE: Maybe the tree stands for something quite different. What is the habitat of a tree, for example?

SARAH: You mean the tree is an individual in a habitat and growing is its moving? Something like that.

MIKE: I don't know. Maybe it doesn't mean an individual at all. Maybe it's a metaphor for branching out, growing up.

ELLEN: Maybe it stands for growing out toward the open, I mean, like open education?

TOM: It's another mystery.

ELLEN: Yes, that's it. The first lesson began with a mystery and the last lesson ends with one.

SARAH: But the episode of the tree itself has a funny ending, a sort of nonending.

MIKE: The tree man calls back?

SARAH: Yes.

ROBERT: Look, you've been having a good time with your mystery, but why make it a mystery? It seems to me you've just been putting meanings into the text. You've just been inventing things.

SARAH: Suppose we have just been inventing things. Then those things are our things. We made them. We learned them. Right? We know more than we did before.

ROBERT: You're still inventing.

ELLEN: You have to admit that inventors have their uses, though.

ROBERT: But not when it comes to education. You can't use children for your inventions. You just don't have that right. Look, you think I'm just absolutely against everything the book stands for. It seems that way, I know, and I said before I feel very strongly that it says some dangerous things. But I'm willing to admit that it does also have a few good points. In one of the early chapters a math lesson is described in which the teacher is helping the children to measure their heights. The conversation is described and a whole range of limitations comes out of the lesson. Then in Chapter Eight, I think it is, height and measurement are again discussed, and I think this is really useful. Incidentally, this may be one of your reflections. But the point I'm trying to make is that I got quite a lot of ideas from the book, and I'm really going to go away and try them.

SARAH: You mean you did find some use in the book after all?

ROBERT: Yes. I just thought of something else, too. You talk about mysteries. I found some strange things. Take, for example, the math incidents I just referred to. No cross reference is made. I don't understand why that second example, in the open class, is not compared with the first. It would drive home the advantages, wouldn't it?

ELLEN: You recognized the advantages. Maybe that was enough.

TOM: Maybe that's just an example of another difference in the systems. You seem to think it would be an advantage. That somehow means you must be thinking competitively. But the new system, whatever, doesn't think that way. It's open. You are free to take it. Its advantages are not advantages if they're compulsive, or compulsory.

ROBERT: Yes, I see that. I guess that says something about me. I really want kids to learn. I really want them to have the best.

ELLEN: But you can't give them these things. They can only take them for themselves.

ROBERT: I guess in a way I know that. But it bothers me that they might take the wrong things, the bad things. I don't want them to learn bad things. I don't see how in the open system they can learn to distinguish. I'm going back to being critical again, but somewhere in the book, again in the math chapter, I think, it says something about not being concerned with learning the New Math or the new anything. I forget the words, but then it says it is concerned "simply with learning." That's what I find so hard to take. Surely we can learn vices as well as virtues, and if the teacher doesn't distinguish, how will the children? If you abandon the curriculum, then surely you abandon all control over what needs to be taught. I see the maintenance of the curriculum as central to teaching. It may not be possible to teach all the good things, but at least you can attempt some of them.

MIKE: If you have a curriculum, you spend most of your time trying to evaluate what's best before you even start to teach.
The great curriculum argument is central to teachers.

ELLEN: I think everyone would sympathize with the dilemma you
are in, Robert, but I'm surprised that you tie in the moral
issue with the curriculum. When you talk about vice and
virtue, you don't really mean that these appear on the curriculum. You seem to be stating two separate arguments,
which for the moment I can't distinguish.

ROBERT: I got carried away, rather, and maybe I didn't make myself
very clear. I guess I'm really concerned about standards, in
work and in behavior. I don't see how you can keep these
up if you've no way of measuring them against some mean.
The curriculum, whatever its limitations, does give you the
possibility of knowing whether the students are really—I
was going to say learning something, but you'd probably
jump on me for that.

ELLEN: I don't want to jump on you, but I'd like to propose some
kind of answer. In the first place, if we can accept what
happens in the book, the basic curriculum, the standard
requirements, whatever, get covered very easily. Children
learn to read and write and count and all the rest of it much
better, or at least as well as they would do by any other
method. So I'm really concerned to answer what I think
may be troubling you much more, the question of standards
of behavior and moral values. My impression is that the
book assumes that learning is good, and it's this assumption
that you are questioning. Is that a fair statement?

ROBERT: Yes, I think it is.

ELLEN: I'd like to take the assumption and try to see how it would
work, because if it won't, then I think your objections will
be valid. They may be valid anyway, but I'd like to see what
we can make of the argument without forcing objections
on it for the moment.

TOM: I'm sorry, but I don't much care for this kind of stuff. We've
lost sight of the practical, and to simply theorize is not going to really help any of us.

ROBERT: Well, what do you propose we do, then?

TOM: Do what it does in the book. Look at the consequences. If they are good, then you keep at it, and if not, then you do something else. It's as simple as that.

ROBERT: But is it? Suppose the consequences are bad, but you don't know it. You can't judge.

TOM: But you can judge. If a flower grows, the gardener must be doing something right. At least he's not doing anything seriously wrong. If the consequences have survival value, they're good.

ROBERT: But survival value for whom?

TOM: For the learners, of course. Who else?

ROBERT: You realize, I hope, what you're getting yourself into.

SARAH: I think survival value has something to do with it, because living has something to do with it. But I think it's more complex. If you start with the given situation, the learner has to choose. This contrasts with the convention where the choice is made by someone else. Right?

ROBERT: Yes.

SARAH: Well, if you choose wisely, you will still leave yourself a number of options open. I hadn't thought of it till now, but this is yet another aspect, I think, of open education. As I was saying, you leave options open. If you choose less wisely, then you leave yourself few options, and if you choose unwisely, you leave yourself no options. You are committed to one course of action, whatever the consequences.

ELLEN: I like that. It fits, too, with the behavior of the teacher in book, doesn't it? There are always lots of possibilities. In fact, they seem to grow. There is a steady increase in the what-more-to-do-next business.

MIKE: If you're committed to one course of action, then you're on the confrontation course. You have to fight. And then you can't learn.

ELLEN: I suppose you could learn that you couldn't learn. And in that sense you would find out from the consequences that you had made a bad choice.

ROBERT: But isn't it the duty of a teacher to prevent students from making that kind of decision?

ELLEN: I think you have an option on that. If you decide to prevent them and fail, then they may have a confrontation with you, because you have closed your options.

ROBERT: I don't see that failure necessarily closes one's options. One thing fails, so you try another.

ELLEN: Only provided you have time for that second choice. And it seems to me that time is running out.

TOM: I haven't built my bridge yet.

ROBERT: Do you think you can?

SARAH: I think you've already crossed it.

TOM: Really? The trouble is, the kids haven't. What I really want is for something to bring them together.

MIKE: They could still build bridges.

SARAH: I don't think that the book seriously means that all teachers interested in open education should set about building bridges in their classrooms. Surely it's what the bridge stands for.

MIKE: The communications bit?

SARAH: Maybe.

ELLEN: These kids of yours sound real tough, as though they've got to prove themselves all the time.

TOM: That's about it.

ELLEN: Can't we put them in a position where they are so obviously the strongest that they don't have to prove themselves?

MIKE: If they're all rivals, that will be difficult.

SARAH: What really gets to tough guys?

MIKE: A woman in tears.

TOM: What am I going to do? put on a fancy costume?

MIKE: Bring in the girl friend.

TOM: Are you crazy! They're rivals, remember?

SARAH: No, no. You don't want a girl. You want something really weak and helpless, something they can be kind to and gentle with. They need to care for something, don't they? So that they'll start caring for one another. Isn't that what we're trying to get at?

TOM: Yeah. You're right. That's got to be it. Oh, you're marvelous. That has really got me started. Oh, yes. Now I see it. This is really the beginning.